Oddballs, Wing-Flappers, & Spinners
Great Paper Airplanes

John Bringhurst

TAB Books
Division of McGraw-Hill, Inc.
Blue Ridge Summit, PA 17294-0850

FIRST EDITION
FIRST PRINTING

©1994 by **TAB Books**.
TAB Books is a division of McGraw-Hill, Inc.

Library of Congress Cataloging-in-Publication Data

Bringhurst, John R.
   Oddballs, wing-flappers & spinners : great paper airplanes / by
John Bringhurst.
     p.   cm.
   Includes index.
   ISBN 0-07-067910-X (pbk.)
   1. Paper airplanes.   I. Title. II. Title: Oddballs, wing
-flappers, and spinners.
TL778.B754 1994
745.592—dc20   93-39160
                                         CIP

Acquisitions editor: Jeff Worsinger
Editorial team: Robert E. Ostrander, Executive Editor
              Norval G. Kennedy, Editor
              Elizabeth J. Akers, Indexer
Production team: Katherine G. Brown, Director
                Susan E. Hansford, Coding
                Jan Fisher, Layout
                Lorie L. White, Proofreading
Design team: Jaclyn J. Boone, Designer
             Brian Allison, Associate Designer   HT1
Cover photograph: Brent Blair, Harrisburg, Pa.   4534

In memory of David C. Willford.

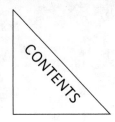

Birds, bugs, and wing-flappers

Oddballs and novelties

Things that spin

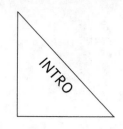

BLEARY-EYED, I stoop in the dark squalor of my dungeon-like study, a blank sheet of paper staring me in the face, while from behind, the fine-honed blade of an editor's deadline stands poised above my skinny neck like the axe in the hairy hand of a black-hooded executioner.

My skin crawls as my mind gropes back to the first paper airplane book—something about planes, jets, and helicopters—and to my heart-wrenching confession that served as introduction to that book. "How am I supposed to follow that?" I mutter. "Another confession? It's only a paper airplane book, after all, just like the first; for that matter, why does it even *need* an introduction?"

"It's another book, it needs another introduction," my editor snarls back from beneath the black hood. "Today!" he adds, in a voice of thunder that rattles the chamber, causing bits of moss and damp earth to rain down about me from the cold stone walls and raftered ceiling.

"All right," I whine, covering my head with my scrawny arms. "I'll write! I'll write!" And still trembling, I clutch my pen miserably and press it to the blank sheet of paper, paper that on a kindlier day I might have sent soaring, dipping gracefully through the open sky.

Crouched thus, with the editor's rough breathing still behind me, I wonder desperately why indeed I have bothered with another book. What is the point? How many paper airplanes need one man make? Was not the first book penance enough for my years of shameless and uncontrolled paper folding?

Yet deep down I know the answer, and I feel that urge, long stifled by civility, still smoldering away inside. It is a thing that never really dies. Even now, from within the darkest twisted

A confession under duress

chambers of my mind comes the mad echo of an insatiable voice that cries, louder and yet louder, "Why not? Why only jets and planes? Why not things that look outlandish? Why not bugs, and bats, and birds? And if birds and bats, why should they not flap their wings? Why should they not flutter or spin, for that matter, or tumble? Why not? WHY NOT?"

And all of a sudden, I realize I am leaping about the cold stone floor, clutching a blank sheet of paper in my sweat-drenched hands with an exhilarated "Why not?" still trembling at my lips. "There," I sigh, "I have done it!" And pausing, I fancy I feel something like a sharp breath of fresh air across the nape of my neck, then hear behind me a low growl from the editor as my head tumbles to the ground and rolls quietly across the study floor . . ..

The rules

Those who have availed themselves of my first book know that I consider the art of paper airplane folding to be governed by certain basic rules (three rules, to be exact) that are followed strictly in this book and that help to bring some semblance of order to the chaos of possibilities that would otherwise certainly result.

Rule #1   Each plane must be folded from a single sheet of paper: 8½ × 11 inches.

Rule #2   Planes must be folded only: no cutting, taping, or gluing.

Rule #3   Every plane must fly, or at least do something interesting in the air.

I am not suggesting that anyone need follow these rules to the exclusion of all other methods, only that I follow them and I suggest them to others as a reasonable set of guidelines under which to work. I have found that even within these limits the possibilities are virtually endless; certainly the designs in this book and the previous volume should offer some convincing evidence of that.

Although the airplane designs in this book venture much farther from the beaten path than those in the first, the same basic principles govern both folding and flying of the majority of the designs. Hence I include here the same basic information about folding and flying that was found in the previous book. It is my hope that most readers will skip over this preliminary material, open the book to a plane they like, and simply start folding—most will find the instructions and illustrations to be self-explanatory, as long as the directions are read and followed carefully. This section is intended for those who have difficulty transforming the instructions into actual folds on a sheet of paper. Recognizing that some people have been tragically deprived of the joys of paper airplane folding and hence might be unaware of the basics, we will first discuss some general guidelines of paper folding simply to make life easier, then follow with some specific types of folds that are frequently used.

Paper folding basics

General guidelines

- Fold your plane on a smooth, flat surface, such as a table or large book. It is very difficult to try to fold on an uneven surface, and nearly impossible using only your hands without a flat surface to fold against.

- Align each fold carefully before creasing, then crease with a smooth motion using your fingertips against the folding surface. If the fold takes the wrong path, you can usually realign it and crease again.

- Follow the directions carefully. Some illustrations have several instructions, and each instruction must be completed before moving on.

- On most planes, the exact placing of any fold is less important than that the folds be made equally on both sides of the plane.

- Be as precise as you can, but don't worry if some folds aren't perfectly accurate—in most cases the plane will fly anyway.

- It is best if you use good paper (these designs were tested with photocopy-quality bond paper), but almost any standard-sized paper will work for most designs, even three-hole binder paper. Generally, the paper you use should be fairly smooth, without folds or crumpled areas.

Folding against an edge

Many of the airplane folds are made using a crease or an edge as a guide. Figures 1–5, for example, show a series of two consecutive diagonal folds against a vertical crease. Note that each fold extends from the top edge where the vertical crease ends; this is where you should start your fold. First, begin the fold at the point marked A in Fig. 1, and holding that position down with your finger, align the top edge AB (between A and B) with the vertical crease, as shown in Fig. 2. Keeping this edge aligned, flatten down and crease the fold from point A diagonally outward to point C, as shown by the arrow.

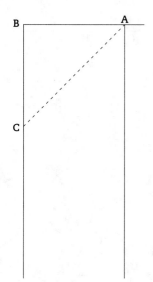

Fig.1 *Folding against a crease.*

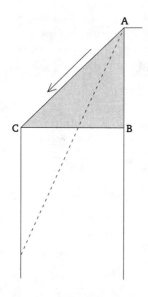

Fig.2 *Folding against a crease.*

Shading represents underside of paper when folded.

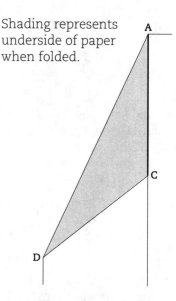

Fig.3 *Folding against a crease.*

The second fold is made the same way. The fold is started at point A, and edge AC is aligned against the central crease as shown in Fig. 3, then holding that edge firmly aligned with one hand, the folded section is flattened down and creased firmly from point A out to point D. This type of fold might take some practice at first if you have not done much paper folding, but it quickly becomes a simple matter.

Sometimes, especially in heavily folded designs, the thickness of the folded paper edges can make further folding difficult; therefore, when making the folds against a crease as shown in Figs. 1–3, it sometimes helps to align the edge a very short distance away from the crease and parallel to it, rather than exactly on it. If you then have to fold along the crease as shown in Figs. 4 and 5, there will be sufficient room for the bulky folded edges and the fold will be much easier and more tidy.

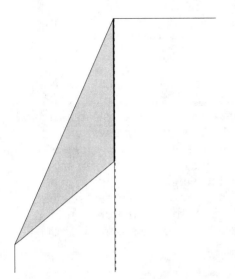

Fig.**4** *Folding against a crease.*

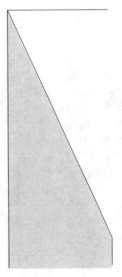

Fig.**5** *Folding against a crease.*

Some folds are created by aligning one point with another point and folding crosswise between them. This type of fold is illustrated in Figs. 6–7. This fold is formed by aligning the tip, labeled A, with point B where the horizontal crease crosses the vertical one. Note that this creates a fold exactly between these two points. Holding the tip down against point B as shown in Fig. 7 with one hand, you first crease flat at point C in the center, then extend the crease to both sides as shown by the arrows.

Folding from point to point

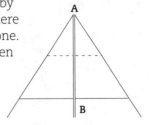

Fig.**6** *Folding from point to point.*

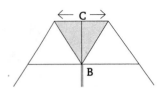

Fig.**7** *Folding from point to point.*

In making such a fold, it is important to keep the center of the plane exactly aligned as shown in Fig. 8. If the fold is made unevenly, as in Fig. 9, subsequent folds will also be uneven and the plane will likely fly poorly.

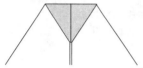 

Fig.**8** *Folded correctly.*   Fig.**9** *Folded incorrectly.*

Accordion folds

Certain planes require one or more accordion folds—that is, folds on which a segment is turned inside-out like the pleats of an accordion. Accordion folds are actually quite simple to form, and an example is shown in Figs. 10–13. Figure 10 shows part of the tail end of an airplane from the side, with the wings folded upward. To form the accordion fold, the end of the tail, marked A, is pushed upward between the wings, causing the folded section AB to turn inside-out, as shown by the dotted section in Fig. 11. The folds from B to C should then be flattened from the sides and creased. Figures 12 and 13 show the same fold from above, with the wings extended.

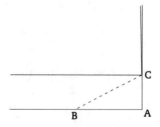 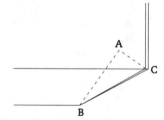

Fig.**10** *Accordion fold.*   Fig.**11** *Accordion fold.*

A few planes require more complex accordion folds, or even complicated telescoping folds; instructions are given for these folds where needed.

Making it fly

Paper has a personality that takes some getting used to, and occasionally a paper plane, however nicely folded, refuses to fly

Fig.**12** *Accordion fold.* Fig.**13** *Accordion fold.*

well. Instructions for many of the airplanes include suggestions for adjustments in case the airplane does not fly well; however, the following general guidelines apply to most planes.

Proper throw

The way a plane is thrown often determines the way it flies. A plane should be thrown with a straight pushing motion (Fig. 14), as you would throw a dart, rather than a curved motion as you would use to throw a baseball (Fig. 15). The speed of the toss is also important; for example, a plane resembling early straight-winged planes will not fly well with a supersonic launching. Each airplane has a "To Fly" paragraph that provides specific instructions on how best to fly that particular plane. A good flight might be a matter of a little practice.

Proper shaping

The plane should be symmetrical—right and left sides should match as exactly as possible. Sight along the center of the plane from back to front to see if the wings match in most details, and make necessary adjustments. It sometimes helps

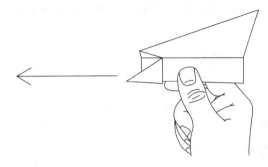

Fig.**14** *Correct toss.*

Introduction xiii

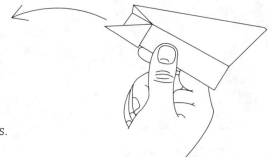

Fig. **15** *Incorrect toss.*

to fold the wings against each other to realign them, and to carefully refold all the edges so they are sharp and exact.

Proper steering   If with careful folding the plane still veers off course, try steering the airplane. Steering a plane is a little like steering a boat, except that whereas a rudder is used behind a boat to steer it right or left, on a paper plane the back edge of the wing is bent to steer the wing up or down. (In some planes, the entire wing can be tilted upward or downward.) This bend is called an *elevator* or *aileron*, and is made as follows:

- If the plane dives into the ground or descends too quickly, bend the back edge of both wings upward slightly. This will cause the plane to climb more.

- If the plane noses up and stalls, do just the opposite—bend the back wing edges down slightly until you get a steady flight.

- If the plane veers off to one side, observe which wing goes up. Slightly bend upward the back edge of that wing, which should make the errant wing tend to dip in flight, straightening the turn. Make another short test flight, readjusting if necessary.

If, with some effort at adjustment, the plane still won't fly, why not just get another piece of paper and try again? It takes little time and effort—that is the beauty of paper airplane folding, after all. Follow the instructions carefully and crease well, and your plane should fly.

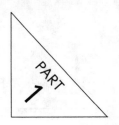

Birds, bugs, and wing-flappers

THE OBJECTIVE of this book is to present designs that are a little more out of the ordinary than the typical paper airplane. This section introduces a group of planes that resemble less the man-made type of aircraft than those that appear in nature: birds, insects, and the like.

It is perhaps not surprising that in many cases, the closer a paper plane comes to resembling these creatures, the more it behaves like them, and this opens an entire menagerie of possibilities to the enterprising folder of paper planes. Here we will introduce a few of the creatures that can be folded and flown, and some of their more unusual and whimsical traits such as wing-flapping, which could perhaps be considered the ultimate animal behavior for a paper airplane.

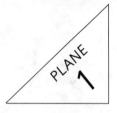

Seagull

THIS FIRST DESIGN IS RELATIVELY SIMPLE and demonstrates some of the basic folding techniques that make a paper airplane birdlike. It is a good plane that flies well, and if you are lucky it might introduce you to the phenomenon of wing-flapping, which is more formally introduced with PLANE 7. (Folding instructions are on pages 3–6.)

To fly Hold the plane from beneath. Toss directly forward and release.

Adjustments The key to adjusting this plane is in the angles of the wing folds in Steps 10, 12, and 13. Sight the plane from behind and make certain that both wings bend exactly the same. In the same way, adjust the angles of the various folds equally until the plane flies well. The wing folds should approximate the shape of a bird's wing, and the plane should look like a bird in flight. Turns to the right or left can be corrected by adjusting the angles of one or both wingtip folds in Step 13. For remarks on wing flapping, see the instructions for PLANE 7.

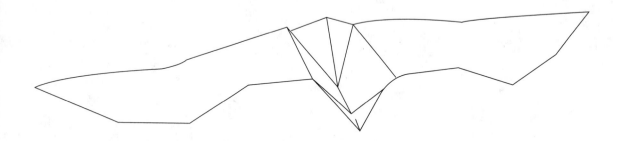

1. With the paper as shown, make a central crease by aligning the left edge of the paper with the right. Crease well.

Unfold.

Turn the paper over.

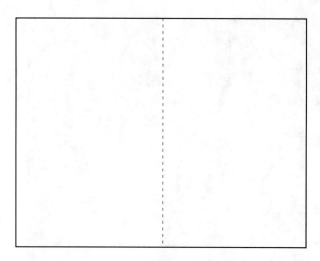

2. Make a diagonal fold as shown by creasing from the right bottom corner, carefully aligning the right edge with the bottom edge of the paper.

Unfold.

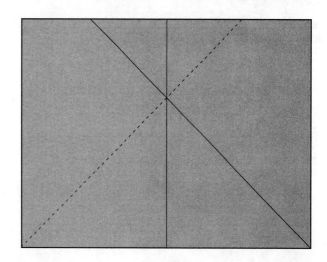

3. Repeat with the left side, folding down the left edge to align with the bottom edge.

Unfold.

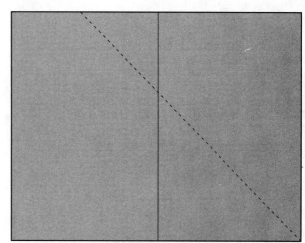

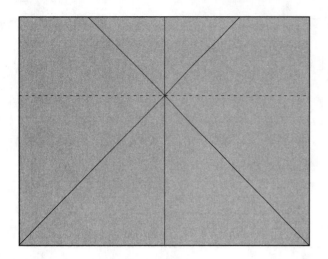

4. Make a horizontal fold, making the fold pass exactly through the intersection of the diagonal and vertical folds, as shown. Make certain to keep the central crease perfectly aligned.

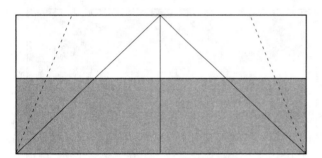

5. Now make a fold on both sides as shown, so that the side edge of the paper aligns with the diagonal crease on each side. The result should look like Fig. 6.

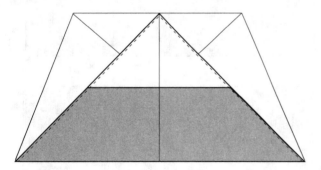

6. Fold down each side along the diagonal crease, as shown.

7. Now make a horizontal fold as shown, so that the tip extends about ½ inch below the base of the paper, as in Fig. 8. Be certain you keep the central crease exactly aligned.

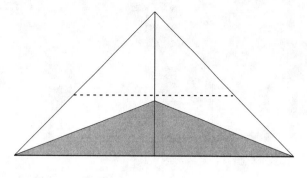

8. Fold the tip back forward, so it extends about ½ inch beyond the front edge. Again, be careful to keep the central crease aligned.

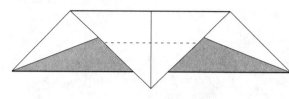

9. Shows the result of Step 8.

Turn the plane over.

Fold in half along the central crease. The wings should match up perfectly, or nearly so.

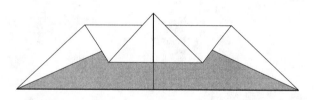

10. Fold down each wing about ¾ inch from the central fold, and parallel to it. Make certain both wings are folded exactly the same.

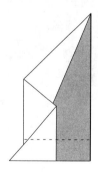

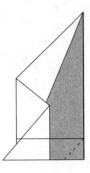

11. Fold up a small tail with an accordion fold, as shown (*see* Fig. 13).

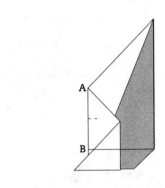

12. Make a small bend in the forward edge of each wing by bringing corner A down to point B on each side.

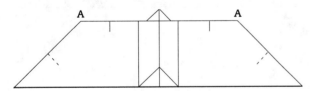

13. This is a top view. Now make a small bend in the diagonal edge of each wing as shown by bending the wingtip forward to corner A on each side, and creasing the front edge slightly. Note that as a result of Steps 12 and 13 the wings bend downward near the body and upward again toward the tip. Make certain that all bends are approximately equal on each side.

Flying instructions for PLANE 1 are on page 2.

Albatross

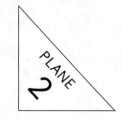

THIS IS ANOTHER DESIGN resembling a bird. With a length of less than 2 inches and a wingspan of nearly 14 inches, it has an impressive wingspread and in appearance at least is the most birdlike design of all. It glides reasonably well if adjusted properly and if nobody opens a door suddenly because a small gust of wind will send this touchy plane out of control. (Folding instructions are on pages 8–12.)

To fly

Hold by the body from beneath, and toss gently directly forward. Indoors this plane can be thrown quite forcefully when adjusted well, but generally it does not do well out-of-doors.

Adjustments

Make certain the wing folds in Steps 11, 13, and 14 are exactly the same on each side. Sight along the center of the plane and make certain the wings are symmetrical. If the plane veers to one side, straighten the flight by increasing the angle of the wingtip bend (from Step 14) on the opposite side, and/or by decreasing the angle on the same side. Periodically recrease the front edge of both wings and re-form the wing bends.

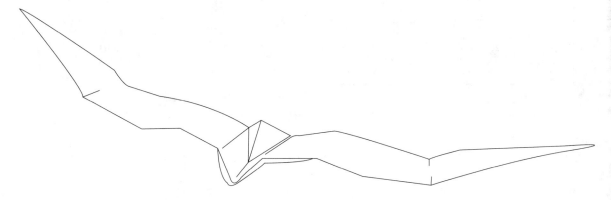

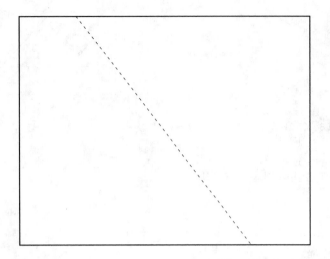

1. Make a diagonal fold as shown by placing the lower left corner of the paper exactly over the upper right corner and creasing well.

Unfold.

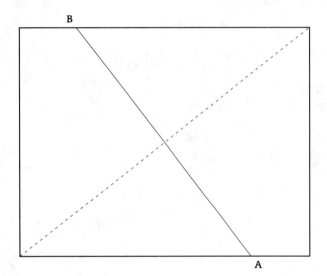

2. Now make another diagonal fold by placing one end of the crease you just made (labeled A) exactly over the other end (labeled B), and creasing. The resulting fold should extend exactly from corner to corner of the paper. (*See* Fig. 3.)

3. Fold down the top left corner of the paper, following the diagonal paper edge exactly as shown.

Fold down the top right corner in exactly the same way, again following the diagonal edge. (Note that on the right, rather than folding over the edge, you are folding away from it.) The result should look like Fig. 4.

4. Now make a horizontal fold through point C as shown, by folding the tip down and aligning it exactly with the central crease. Crease well.

5. Make a diagonal crease as shown from each lower corner to the front end of the central crease, following the paper edge on each side.

Unfold.

6. Now fold down each side starting at the bottom corner as shown, aligning the edge with the diagonal crease you just made.

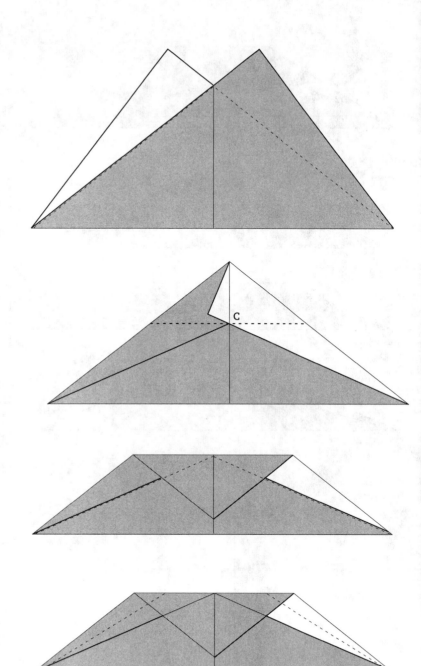

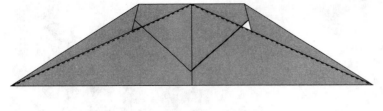

7. Fold again on each side along the diagonal crease. By this time the front edges of the wings will be quite thick, so crease very well.

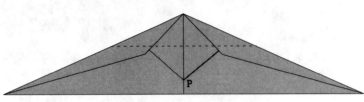

8. Shows the result of Step 7. Now fold the tip of the plane down so it just touches the point of paper labeled P. Crease the front fold very well.

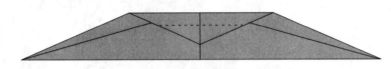

9. Fold the tip forward, so that it protrudes just beyond the front edge of the plane as shown. Make certain to keep the central crease lined up.

10. Shows the result of Step 9. Turn the plane over.

Fold in half along the central crease. The two wings should align exactly against each other.

11. Fold down each wing about ¾ inch from the central crease and parallel with it. Make certain the wings align exactly against each other.

12. Fold up a tail in an accordion fashion—lift the tip of the tail upward and forward between the sides of the body, and creasing. (*See* Fig. 15 for a top view.)

13. With the wings folded upward, grasp both wings together at the point shown, about halfway between corner A and point B. Push each wing outward at that point, forming a distinct downward bend in the forward edge of each wing.

Fold the wings to the downward position, as in Fig. 14.

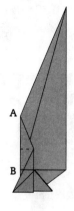

14. Make a small crease in the front of each wing at the point shown by bending the wingtip forward to touch the nose of the plane. Crease only the very front of the wing, and unfold. This should make the wingtips point upward slightly.

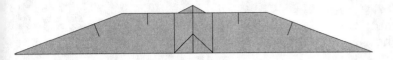

15. Shows the finished plane from above.

Flying instructions for PLANE 2 are on page 7.

Owl

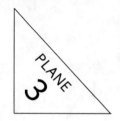

FOR A CHANGE OF PACE, this bird is simple to fold and easy to fly, with a smooth, stable glide. In flight, it reminds me of the nighttime ventures of a pale barn owl that used to occupy a tree in our backyard. (Folding instructions are on pages 14–18.)

To fly

Hold from beneath and throw gently forward. Although this is a good indoor flier, it may be thrown outside if there is not too strong a breeze; however, you must use a gentle toss, and it flies better if thrown with the wind rather than against it. If you toss the plane gently upward you can achieve a longer flight outdoors.

Adjustments

The angle of the wings is all-important. The wings should bend upward from the body at the same angle on each side, and the slight downward bend at midwing should also be the same on both sides. If it still does not fly well, try recreasing all edges, and readjust the wing folds.

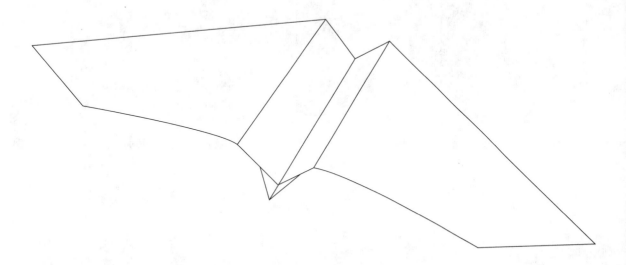

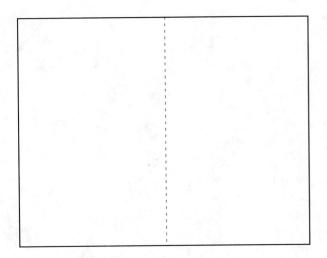

1. With the paper as shown, make a central crease by aligning the left edge of the paper with the right.

Unfold.

Turn the paper over.

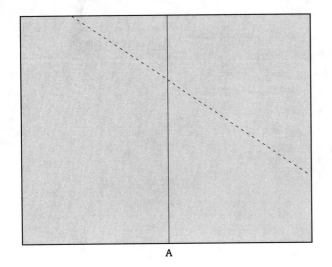

A

2. Make a diagonal fold as shown by placing the right upper corner of the paper over point A at the bottom center of the paper, and creasing.

Unfold.

3. Make a similar crossing diagonal fold by placing the left upper corner against point A and creasing again.

Unfold. If you did Step 2 and 3 carefully, the three creases should cross at the same point, as shown.

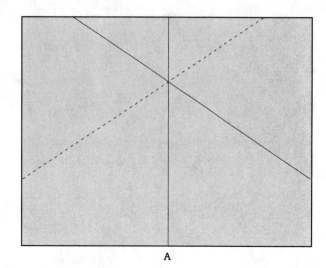

A

4. Fold up the bottom corner on each side, so that the outer edge is aligned against the diagonal creases you just made, as shown in Fig. 5. Crease well.

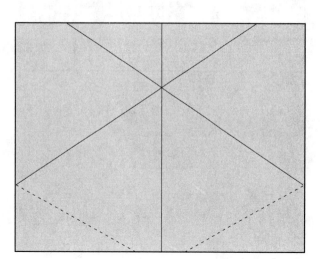

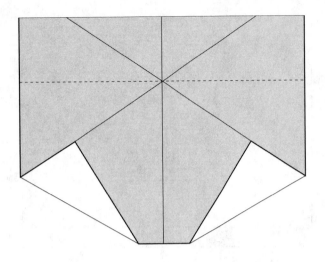

5. Now fold down the top edge of paper, so that the fold passes exactly through the point shown, where the creases intersect. Be certain to keep the central crease aligned.

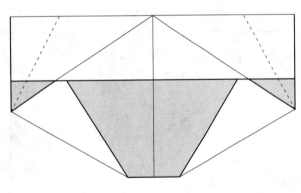

6. Shows the result of Step 5. Now make a fold on each side as shown, in each case aligning the outer edge with the diagonal crease. The result should look like Fig. 7.

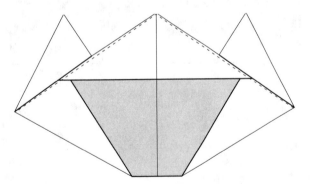

7. Fold down each side along the diagonal crease. The result should look like Fig. 8.

8. Note that there is a horizontal edge of paper in the center. Fold down along this horizontal edge, folding down the tip so that it rests exactly along the central crease. Crease the resulting top edge very well.

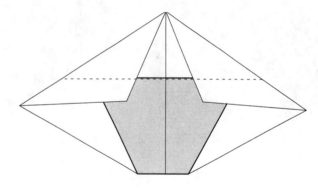

9. Now fold the tip forward so that it protrudes about ¼ inch beyond the front of the plane. Make certain the central crease is exactly aligned, and crease well.

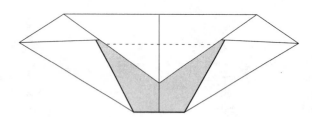

10. Shows the result. Turn the plane over.

Fold in half along the central crease.

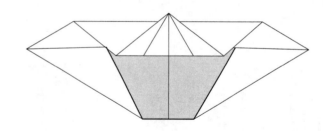

11. Fold down the wings as shown. The fold should be roughly parallel to the body, and extend to corner P in the back. (The exact location of the fold is of little importance, so long as both wings are folded exactly the same.) Unfold.

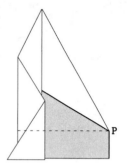

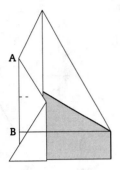

12. With the wings folded upward, grasp the wings together at the point shown midway between A and B, and bend each wing gently outward.

Flying instructions for PLANE 3 are on page 13.

Falcon

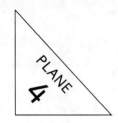
A STRIKING DESIGN, the Falcon is challenging to fold but can be made to fly very well. It is not too difficult if you follow directions carefully. (Folding instructions are on pages 20–23.)

To fly

Hold the body from beneath, and launch directly forward with a moderate throw.

Adjustments

This is a bulky plane, so see that the edges are creased as flat as possible. The folds on the wings are very important, and should match each other exactly on each side. Adjust also the angle of the wings themselves, so that they angle up from the body equally on each side. If more lift is required, bend the tips of the tails upward slightly.

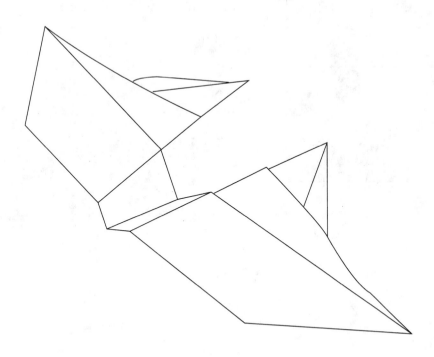

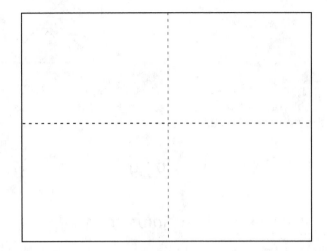

1. Make a vertical central crease by folding the left edge of the paper flush against the right. Crease well.

Unfold.

Make a similar horizontal crease by folding the bottom edge flush with the top edge. Crease well.

Unfold.

Turn the paper over.

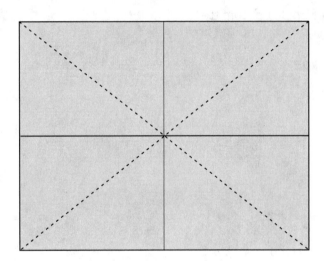

2. Now make crisscrossing corner-to-corner folds as shown (this is more difficult than it looks). Fold first one diagonal, unfold, then fold the other.

Unfold the paper flat.

3. Now make a complex accordion fold—lift the points labeled A on each side and bring them toward the center on the bottom. The paper should fold naturally along all the diagonal creases, bringing the two top corners directly over the bottom corners.

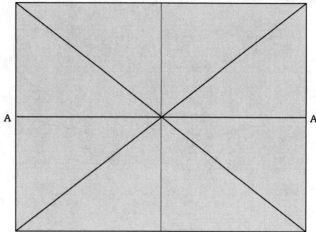

4. Shows the fold in progress. Note that two sets of wings have been formed, one directly over the other. Aligning the top set of wings exactly with the bottom set, crease the diagonal folds flat. The result should look like Fig. 5.

5. Now fold the topmost wing on each side inward, so that the diagonal edge extends from the front tip to the corner marked P on each side. Crease well.

Unfold each side.

Refold along the same fold, but this time in the opposite direction, turning the ends of the wings under, so the edge rests in the slot ending at point P on each side (*see* Fig. 6).

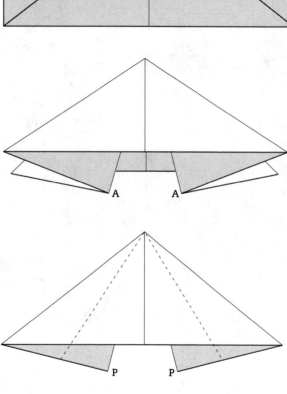

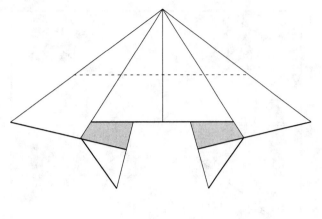

6. Shows the result of the previous fold. Now fold down the tip so that it extends about ¾ inch below the horizontal edge at the bottom of the plane. (*See* Fig. 7.) Make certain the central crease is aligned before creasing.

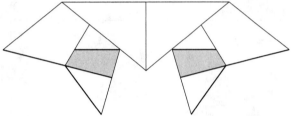

7. Shows the result of Step 6. Unfold.

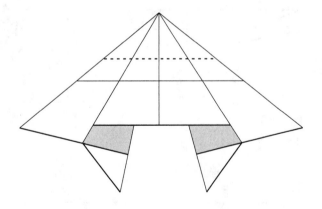

8. Fold the tip down again so that the horizontal crease you just made in Step 6 lies about midway between the front edge and the tip, as shown in Fig. 7. Keep the central crease exactly aligned.

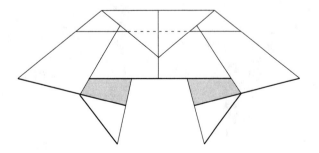

9. Now fold down along the horizontal crease as shown. Crease very well because this forms the front of the airplane.

10. Shows the result of Step 9. Turn the plane over.

Fold in half along the central crease.

At this point you will notice the plane is quite bulky. Flatten all edges firmly between your fingers, taking care to keep the wings exactly matched.

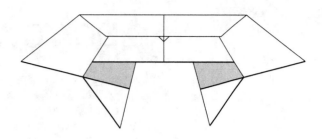

11. Fold down each wing along the line shown. Make certain that both wings are folded exactly the same.

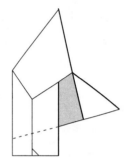

12. Grasp both wings together at about the point marked P; bend the front end of each wing downward. The wings will form a natural bend, as shown. Do not crease.

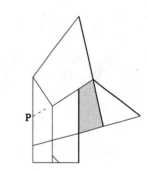

13. This shows the plane from above. Now make a small upward crease on each wing as shown, by folding the tip of each wing to corner C on each side.

Flying instructions for PLANE 4 are on page 19.

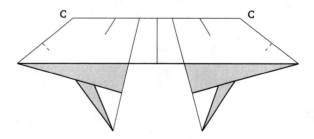

PLANE 5

Sparrow

A SMALL, QUICK FLIER, this plane is a favorite of mine. Folding it is a challenge, to be sure, but it is unique, with a rapid, bobbing flight that makes it resemble its namesake. It can be thrown out-of-doors, where it swoops and bobs as though it were alive. (Folding instructions are on pages 25–30.)

To fly Hold from beneath, and throw briskly forward. This plane will generally fly better with a strong throw than with a gentle toss. You might need to make your throw upward. Outdoors, throw upward firmly.

Adjustments The plane might dive into the ground at first; therefore, before bending elevators, try flattening the front edges of the plane as much as possible, and elevating the wings somewhat so that they angle upward from the body in flight. If it still dives after you make the adjustment, gently bend up an elevator on the back edge of both wings, or bend the back of both sides of the tail inward.

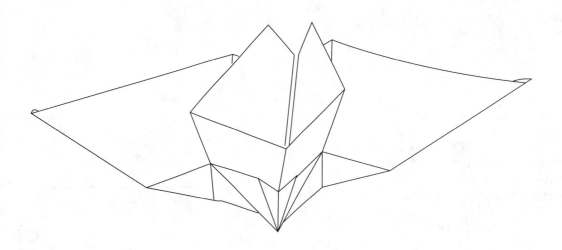

1. Make a crease in the center as shown by folding the bottom edge of the paper flush with the top.

Unfold.

2. Fold down the top of the paper so that it lies flush with the horizontal crease you made in Step 1.

3. Now make a vertical crease, folding the paper in half so that the sides line up exactly.

Unfold.

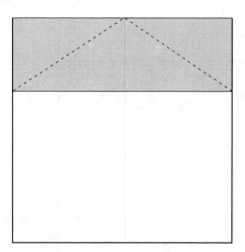

4. Make a diagonal fold on each side, extending from the top of the central crease to the point shown on each side. The result should look like Fig. 5.

5. Now fold down along the paper edge as shown. Make certain you keep the central crease lined up exactly.

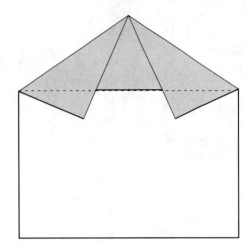

6. Placing the paper as shown, fold the paper over the right diagonal edge, creasing only as far as the tip at point P, as in Fig. 7. Hold down the folded over sheet firmly with your left hand.

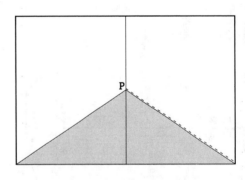

7. Without creasing any farther, fold the right side of the plane over, aligning point A with point B. The paper should fold along the dotted line from point P downward. Crease along this fold.

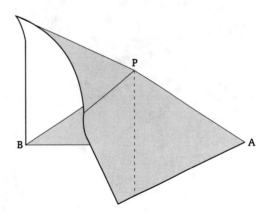

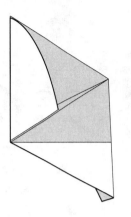

7A. Shows the result of Step 7. Unfold the last two folds, so the paper appears as in Fig. 8.

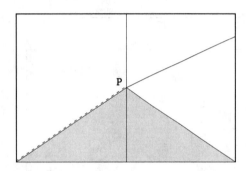

8. Now fold the paper down over the left diagonal edge in the same way as you did on the right in Step 6, again creasing no farther than point P. Hold the folded-over sheet down firmly with your right hand.

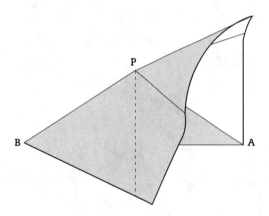

9. Now fold the left side over to the right, aligning point B with point A as in Step 7. Crease as indicated by the dotted line, from the tip downward.

Unfold the last two folds, opening the paper out as in Fig. 9A.

9A. Bring point A and point B downward to the center. The paper will fold naturally along the diagonal creases as shown. The results should look like Fig. 10.

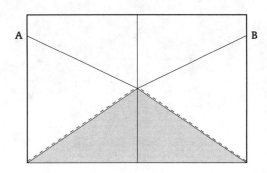

10. Holding the two lower sides together at point W, press the center of the upper edge of paper labeled Q down against the central crease, and flatten the entire upper section, creasing the edges as shown in Fig. 11.

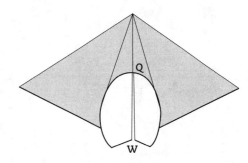

11. The result should look like this. Now fold back the tip so that it just touches the center edge of paper at point Q. Crease very well.

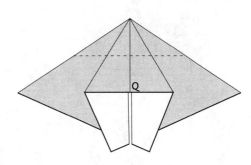

12. Fold the tip forward so that it just protrudes beyond the front edge of the airplane, as in Fig. 13.

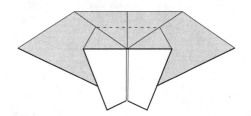

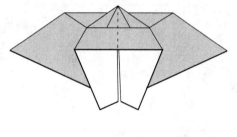

13. Fold in half along the central crease. The wings should match almost exactly.

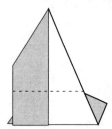

14. Fold down each wing as shown, just over an inch from the central fold. (*See also* Fig. 15.)

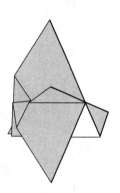

15. The wing should be folded on each side so that the small flap of paper shown remains sticking upward from the body of the plane. Fold both wings exactly the same.

Flying instructions for PLANE 5 are on page 24.

Condor

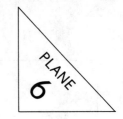
Aɴᴏᴛʜᴇʀ ᴅᴇsɪɢɴ ᴡɪᴛʜ ᴀ ʟᴏɴɢ ᴡɪɴɢsᴘᴀɴ, this plane looks stunningly birdlike in the air. A reliable flier, it is also not particularly difficult to fold. (Folding instructions are on pages 32–35.

To fly

With the wings angled slightly upward from the body, hold from beneath by the body, and toss directly forward. The toss can be quite firm for this plane. Although it will fly outside on a windless day, the plane performs better indoors, where it will give long, smooth flights.

Adjustments

Be certain that the wing bends in Steps 9, 10, and 11 are as equal as possible on both wings. If the plane seems to keel over to one side, try increasing the wingtip bend on that same side to even out the flight. From time to time, recrease the forward edge of each wing and readjust the wing bends.

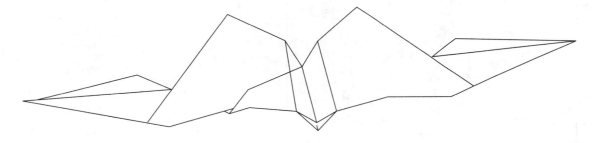

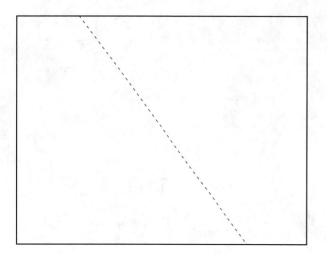

1. Make a diagonal crease as shown by aligning the left lower corner of the paper with the right upper corner. Crease well.

Unfold.

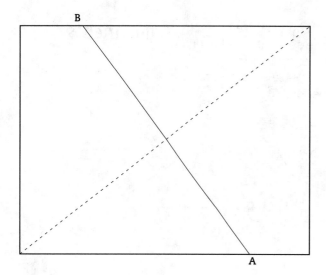

2. Make another diagonal fold perpendicular to the first, by placing one end (marked A) of the crease you just made exactly over the other end (marked B) and creasing. This fold should pass exactly from corner to corner as shown.

3. Placing the paper as shown, make a diagonal fold from the left corner by folding the long bottom fold forward and aligning it with the long edge ending at corner A. Be certain the crease passes exactly through the left lower corner, and crease well.

Unfold.

Make another similar crease from the right lower corner by folding the long bottom fold forward and aligning it with the long edge ending at corner B. Again, make certain your fold passes through the right lower corner, and crease well.

Unfold. If you are careful, the two diagonal creases should cross in the exact center.

Turn the paper over.

4. Fold up the bottom of the paper along the line shown. Your fold should pass exactly through the intersection of the diagonal folds, and the central crease should be perfectly aligned. Crease the bottom edge well.

Rotate the paper to the position shown in Fig. 5.

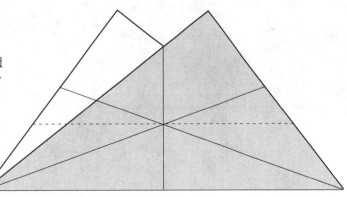

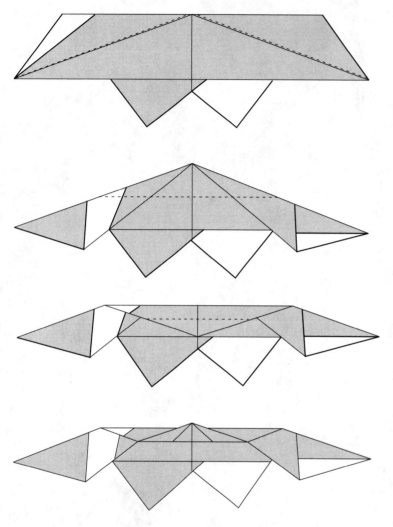

5. Now fold down each side along the diagonal crease. Your fold should extend from the front center of the plane to the wingtip on each side.

6. Shows the result of Step 5. Now fold down the front tip so that it just touches the bottom horizontal edge in the exact center, as in Fig. 7. Recrease the front edge of both wings from the center outward (the creases may shift somewhat).

7. Now fold the tip forward again, so that it protrudes just beyond the front of the plane. Keep the central crease aligned.

8. Shows the result. Now turn the plane over.

Fold in half along the central crease, keeping the wings carefully aligned with each other.

9. Fold down each wing about ½ inch from the central fold and parallel with it. Be certain you fold both wings exactly the same.

Unfold.

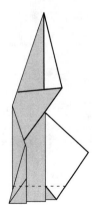

10. Holding the wings together at about the point shown, bend each wing downward, forming a small downward bend in the forward edge of each wing.

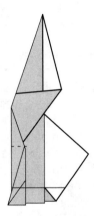

11. This is the plane from above. Bend up each wingtip along the edge shown. Do not crease.

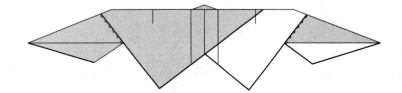

Flying instructions for PLANE 6 are on page 31.

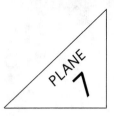

Basic wing-flapper

YOU DID READ IT CORRECTLY—this plane actually does flap its wings in flight, with a little patience and luck. The mechanics of this are beyond me, but no matter, it's fun to watch and it's almost hard to believe your eyes when you get a good flight and see it for yourself. (Folding instructions are on pages 38–41.)

Before proceeding, a word about wing-flappers generally. Wing-flapping is fairly intelligent behavior for a paper airplane, and as a result these planes are temperamental, and tend to flap their wings only when it suits their fancy, not necessarily on demand. Sometimes they seem downright malicious, refusing to perform for guests, then giving flight after flight of matchless wing-flapping after everyone has gone home. This particular design is quite reliable, however, and with some coaxing and patience the results can be truly amazing.

The tendency to flap the wings depends upon several factors. A strong throw increases the tendency to flap, as does the use of a lighter paper, such as *spirit duplicator paper*. Heavy paper might need to be *softened* (described in the Adjustments subsection) before a plane will flap its wings. If you store your airplane flat for a while, the wings will soften with time and tend to flap much more. Very strong wing-flapping can spoil a plane's lift and makes for a weak flight—the trick is to strike a balance between a good flight and a convincing wing-flap. This becomes an art in itself.

To fly Hold from beneath by the body, and toss directly forward. (Note that the pointed end faces backwards.) If the plane tends to flap its wings too much, it may be launched by placing your index finger above, pointed forward in the slot between the wings, and the rest of the hand beneath. Toss forward, and release. Although most reliable indoors, I have launched this plane out-of-doors with a vigorous upward toss; it will often right itself and glide to the ground, flapping all the way.

See that both wings are angled up slightly from the body. If the flapping is too vigorous or the plane flies into the ground, hold it by the forward folded edge and lever the back edge of both wings upward gently. Then try another toss. The back points of the wings can also be bent slightly upward to counteract a tendency to dive. A tendency to turn to one side or the other is usually due to the wings being at different angles with respect to each other. Refold and recrease the wings, making them as symmetric as possible.

If a plane flies well but does not flap its wings, you might need to soften the wings so that they are less stiff and more prone to flap. This can be done by folding and unfolding each wing vigorously many times, or by folding the wing and body inside out then right-side out several times. An even better way to soften the wings is to store the plane flat for a while. (If you have planes that fly well, try putting them away in a manila folder for a few days, taking care not to bend the edges. When you are in the mood, take them out and readjust them, and see how they fly.)

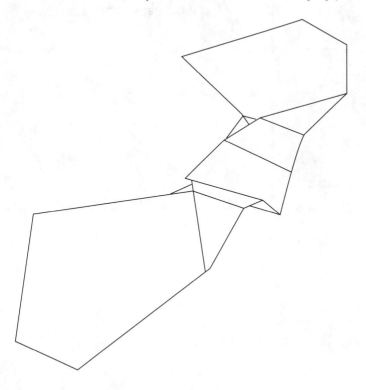

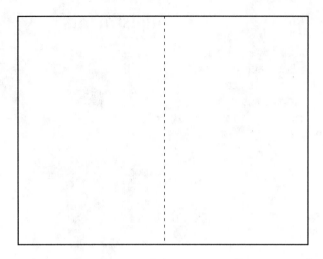

1. With the paper as shown, make a central crease by aligning the left edge of the paper with the right.

Unfold.

Turn the paper over.

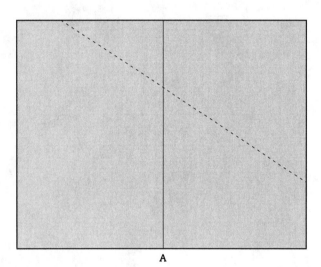

A

2. Make a diagonal fold as shown by placing the right upper corner of the paper over point A at the bottom center of the paper, and creasing.

Unfold.

3. Make a similar crossing diagonal fold by placing the left upper corner against point A and creasing again.

Unfold. If you did Step 2 and 3 carefully, the three creases should cross at the same point, as shown.

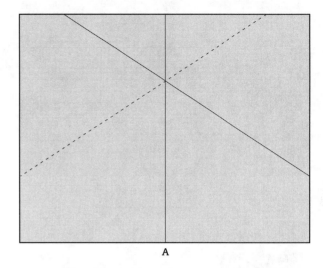

A

4. Now fold down the top edge of paper, so that the fold passes exactly through the point shown, where the creases intersect. Be certain to keep the vertical central crease aligned.

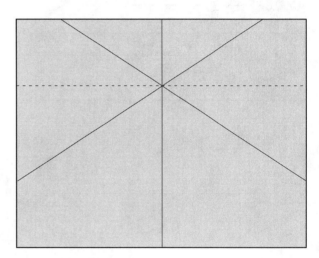

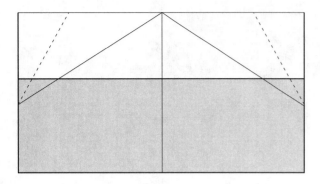

5. Shows the result of Step 4. Now make a fold on each side as shown, in each case aligning the outer edge with the diagonal crease. The result should look like Fig. 6.

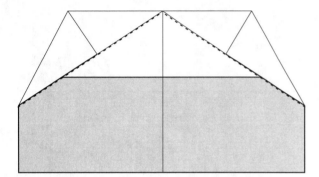

6. Fold down each side along the diagonal crease.

Rotate the paper so that it is in the point-down position shown in Fig. 7.

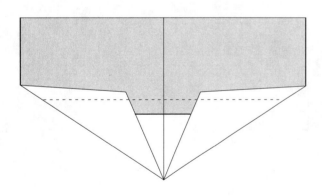

7. Fold up the tip so that it touches the top edge of the paper in the exact center.

8. Now fold down the top paper corner on each side, creasing it tightly against the diagonal edges as shown. The result should look like Fig. 9.

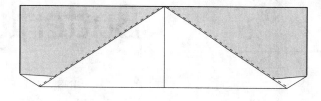

9. Fold the tip downward so that it protrudes about ½ inch below the horizontal paper edge, as shown in Fig. 10. Be certain to keep the midline fold exactly aligned.

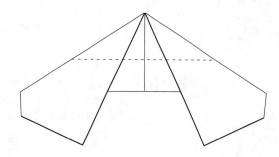

10. Fold in half along the central crease. Be certain the two wings align with each other exactly.

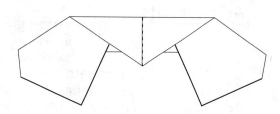

11. Fold down each wing as shown, about 1½ inches from the central crease, carefully aligning the wings with each other. Crease well.

Unfold.

Holding the central fold between thumb and forefinger, bend down each wing slightly at the point indicated by the arrows.

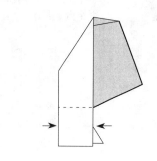

Flying instructions for PLANE 7 are on page 36.

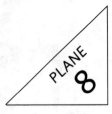

Butterfly

ANOTHER INSECTLIKE DESIGN that really does resemble a butterfly when you get it flying well, this plane flaps its wings quite convincingly if you fold it from a light grade of paper, or if it is kept in storage for a while. (Folding instructions are on pages 43–48.)

To fly   Hold from below with the straight edge of the wing facing forward. Toss directly forward. The plane tends to float as a butterfly, and can be made to flap its wings. It should generally be flown indoors.

Adjustments   If the plane tends to dive, bend the pointed back edge of the wings upward equally on each side. If it tends to bank to one side, try increasing the downward bend of the wingtip on the same side (*see* Step 16). First make certain the wings are symmetrical; you can often straighten out a bad turn simply by matching the bends on the wings exactly. This plane tends to flap its wings very well, but often requires softening as described for PLANE 7. Storing the plane for a while makes for excellent wing flapping.

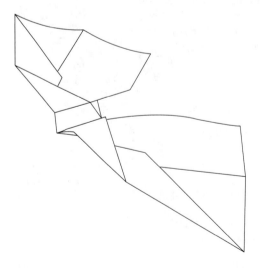

1. With the paper as shown, make a long horizontal crease by aligning the bottom edge of paper exactly with the top, and creasing well in the center.

Unfold.

2. Fold down the top corner on each side as shown, aligning the side edge exactly with the horizontal crease.

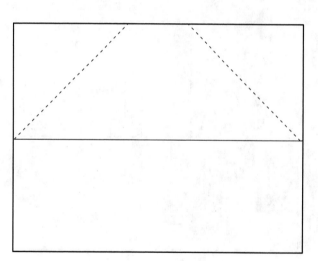

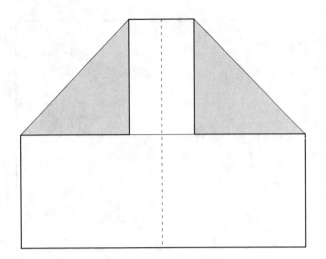

3. Make a central crease as shown by aligning the right edge of the paper exactly with the left and creasing well in the center.

Unfold.

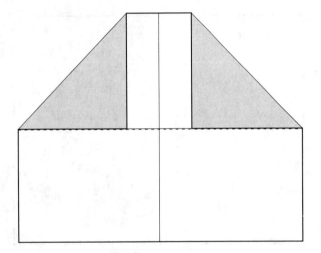

4. Fold the bottom of the paper forward over the top, along the horizontal crease, as shown.

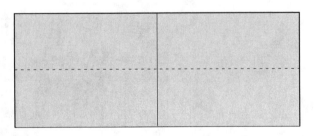

5. Fold the topmost layer of paper down horizontally as shown, aligning the top edge exactly with the bottom fold. Be certain to keep the central crease aligned and crease well.

5A. Shows the result. Unfold the last fold upward.

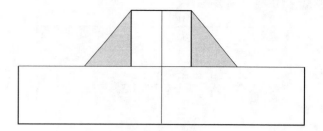

6. Now make a fold starting from the right lower corner as shown, so that the top edge (when folded down) runs exactly across point A in center bottom, as shown in Fig. 7.

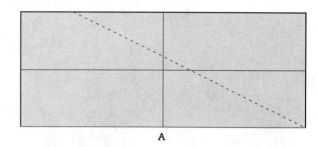

A

7. Shows the result of Step 6. Note where the folded-down edge lies with respect to point A.

Unfold this fold after creasing well.

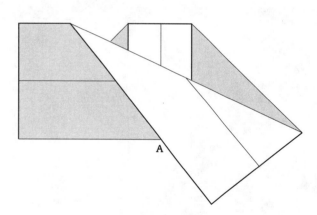

A

8. Form a similar fold starting in the left lower corner, again aligning the folded down top edge with point A.

Unfold. If you did Steps 6, 7, and 8 correctly, the diagonal creases should cross in the exact center, as shown in Fig. 9.

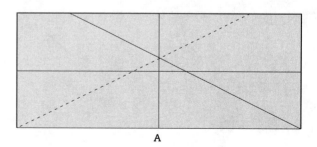

A

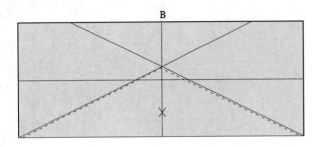

9. Begin to fold the top of the paper toward you, folding along both diagonal creases, as shown.

While this fold is in progress, take the point where the central crease meets the top edge (marked B) and bring it down so that it lies exactly over the central crease in the spot marked X.

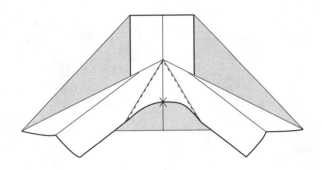

10. Holding the edge down as shown at point X, continue to fold the wings downward along the diagonal creases, as shown.

Continuing to press down at point X, flatten down the wings well, pressing from the front edge backward and from the center out. Note that the paper will fold under as denoted by the dotted lines. The result should look like Fig. 11.

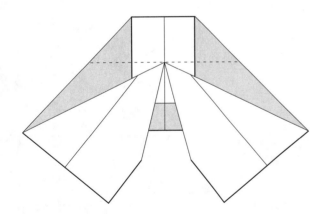

11. Now fold down the top edge as shown over the tip of the lower half of the plane. Be certain you keep the central crease aligned, and crease well.

12. Fold down as shown over the front diagonal edges of the wings on each side.

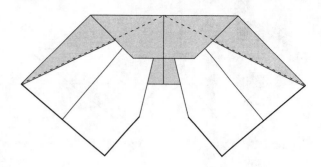

13. Shows the result of Step 12. Now fold the tip downward so that it touches the bottom edge in the exact center. Keep the central crease aligned, and crease very well.

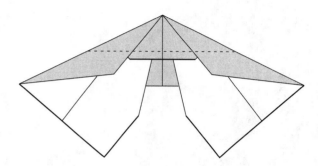

14. The plane should look like this. Fold in half along the central crease, taking care to match the wings to each other exactly.

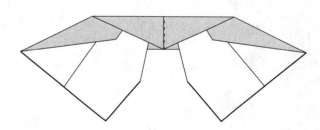

15. Fold down the wings as shown, keeping your fold parallel to the central fold. Match the two wings exactly as you fold.

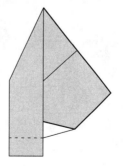

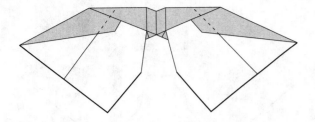

16. This is a top view. Note that there is a diagonal crease in each wing. Bend the forward edge of both wings downward slightly so that they follow the same contour as the crease, as shown.

Flying instructions for PLANE 8 are on page 42.

Moth

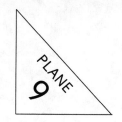

THIS IS ANOTHER VARIATION on the insect theme, which flies very well and can be finished several ways for a variety of effects. When the wings flap, as they will on occasion, they tend to make a rapid flutter. (Folding instructions are on pages 51–53.)

To fly

Hold from beneath. Toss firmly straight forward. This bug, like most others, flies better indoors than out. A stiff throw will sometimes produce a fluttering sort of wing-flapping initially.

Adjustments

This plane has entirely different characteristics, depending upon which final fold is used. The fold shown in Fig. 7 will give you a quick flight with a fluttering flap of the wings. Folded as in Fig. 7A, the plane has a broad, appealing wingspan and will glide smoothly. Folded as in 7B, it will swoop on its swept-back wings. In each case, see that both wings are folded exactly the same. If the plane tends to nose into the ground, simply bend the back edge of each wing gently upward.

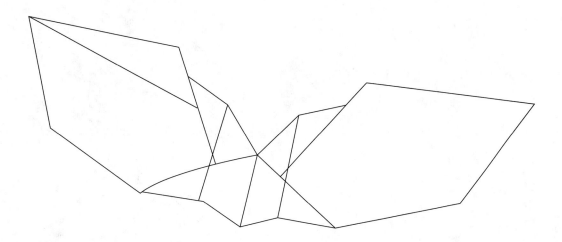

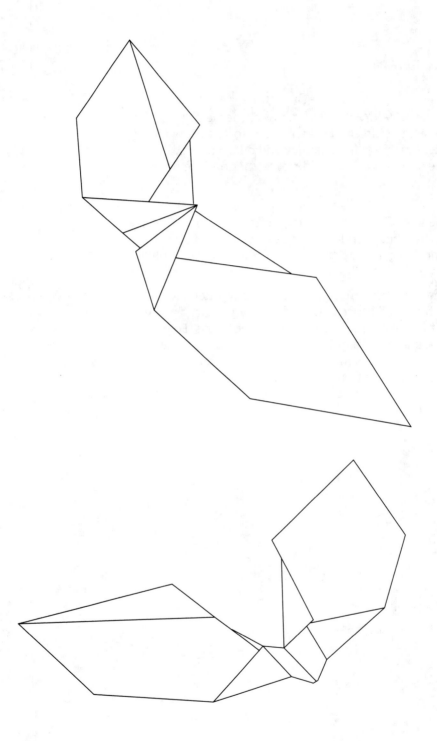

50 Moth

1. Make a diagonal fold as shown by aligning the lower left corner with the upper right, and creasing well.

Unfold.

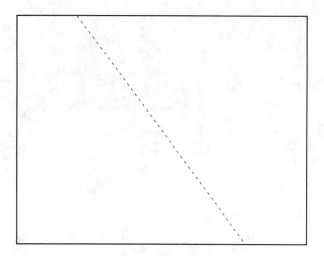

2. Make a fold perpendicular to the first by matching the opposite ends of the crease you just made, labeled A and B, and creasing well. The fold should extend from one corner to the corner opposite, as shown.

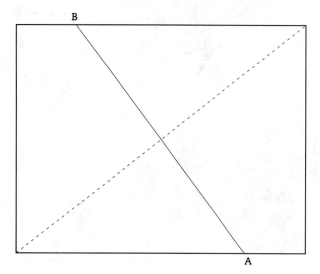

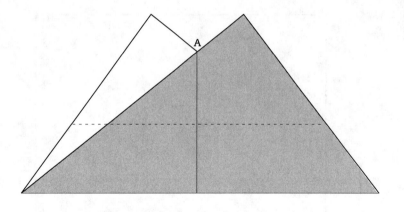

3. Now fold the bottom edge forward so that it touches point A where the two paper edges cross. Make certain you keep the central crease aligned, and crease very well.

Turn the paper over and position it as in Fig. 4.

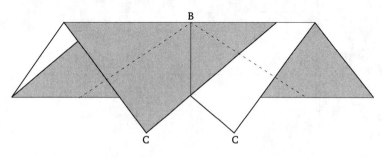

4. Fold down a wing on each side, as shown. You should fold diagonally on each side from point B on the front center, bending over the top edge so it just touches corner C on each side, as shown in Fig. 5. Crease well.

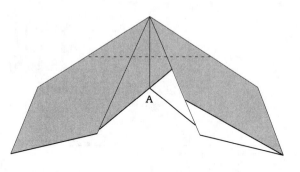

5. Shows the result of Step 4. Now bend the tip downward to point A, making certain to keep the central crease aligned. Crease very well along the front edge, and crease the front edge of both wings outward from the center.

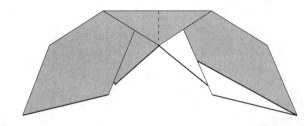

6. Shows the result. Fold in half along the central crease, taking care to match the wings exactly to each other.

7. Fold down each wing as shown, about ½ inch to 1 inch from the central fold and parallel to it. Make certain you fold both wings exactly the same. (For variation, you can fold as shown in Fig. 7A or in Fig. 7B—in each case, both wings should be folded exactly the same.)

Flying instructions for PLANE 9 are on page 49.

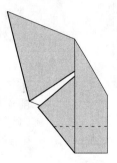

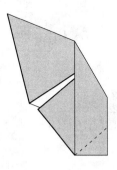

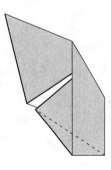

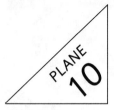
Bat

THIS ANIMAL-LIKE DESIGN BEGGED to be included in the book. Perhaps the most convincing wing-flapper of all, it will sometimes overdo it and flap to the ground like a wounded duck. If you have as yet been unable to get a plane to flap its wings, try this one— although it requires some patience to fold, it is not particularly difficult. (Folding instructions are on pages 55–59.)

To fly

Hold the body from beneath. Toss firmly forward. When the plane is well adjusted, you can give it a vigorous toss and it will almost take on a life of its own, alternately darting and flapping its wings.

Adjustments

First of all, make certain the plane is folded symmetrically and that the wings have the same angles to the air. If necessary, crease the fronts of one or both wings or alter the angles of the folds as needed.

The adjustments in Step 16 are crucial to wing flapping. The downward bend at the front of each wing increases the tendency to flap. (Bending upward rather than downward here will stabilize the flight, but decrease wing-flapping.) The upward bend at the back edge of the wings counteracts a tendency to dive into the ground. Adjust these two bends as needed until you have a satisfactory flight with good flapping action. If the plane tends to fly into the ground, you can hold the body from beneath with one hand, and with the other hand lever the back of each wing upward gently. This will give the plane lift, but might decrease the wing flapping.

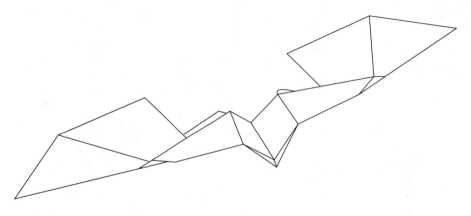

1. With the paper as shown, make a vertical central crease by aligning the left side of the paper with the right.

Unfold.

2. Now make a horizontal central crease as shown by aligning the bottom edge of the paper with the top and creasing between them. Make certain the vertical crease is aligned with itself.

Unfold.

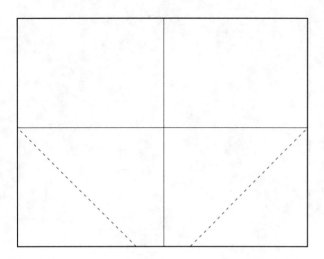

3. Fold up the bottom corner on each side, aligning the side edge of the paper with the horizontal crease, as shown in Fig. 4.

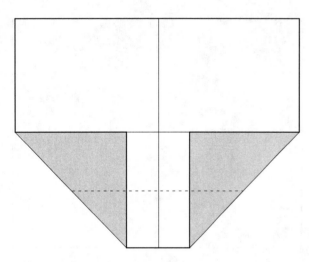

4. Fold up the bottom central edge of the paper, aligning it with the horizontal central crease. Crease well. The result should look like Fig. 5.

5. Make a diagonal fold on each side as shown, aligning the diagonal edge on each side with the horizontal crease as shown in Fig. 6.

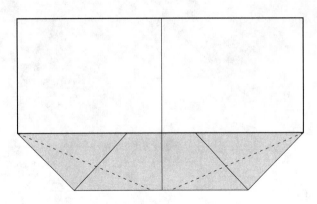

6. Shows the result of Step 5. Fold the top half of the paper over the bottom, along the horizontal crease.

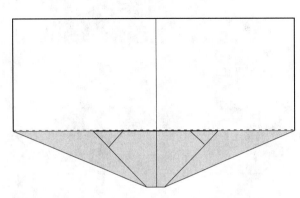

7. Fold the free bottom edge of the paper upward, aligning it exactly with the folded top edge. Make certain the central crease is perfectly aligned with itself, and crease well.

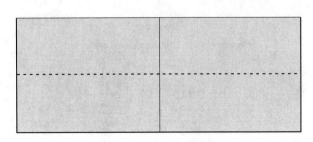

8. Now fold down the top free corner on each side as shown. Your fold should extend from the top of the central crease to the lower corner on each side. When you have the fold lined up well, crease well.

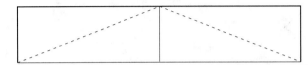

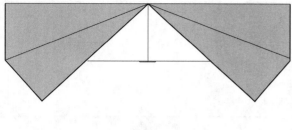

9. Shows the result of Step 8. Turn the paper over, and position it as in Fig. 10.

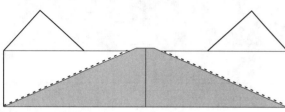

10. Fold the wings over as shown, creasing tightly over the diagonal edge on each side. The result should look like Fig. 11.

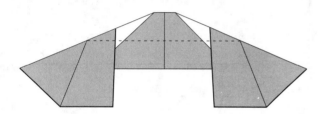

11. Now fold the top central edge down flush with the bottom edge, keeping the central crease exactly aligned. Crease the front edge very well, creasing also the forward edge of the wings on each side, from the center outward. (The folds might shift a little.)

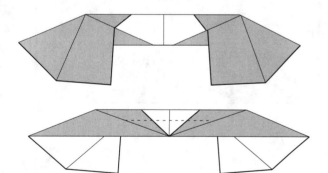

12. Shows the result of Step 11. Turn the plane over.

13. Note that there is a tip pointing downward in the center. Fold this tip forward so that it protrudes slightly more than ¼ inch beyond the front of the plane. Keep the central crease aligned.

14. Shows the result. Turn the plane over.

Fold in half along the central crease, taking care that the wings align exactly with each other.

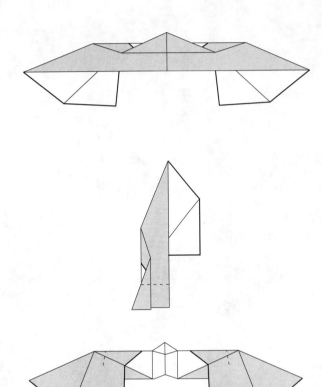

15. Fold down the wing on each side, a little less than 1 inch from the central fold and parallel to it. Make certain both wings are folded exactly alike.

16. Shows the finished plane from above. Bend down the front end of each wing slightly at about the point and angle shown.

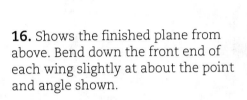

Form a slight elevator by bending up the back end of each wing slightly at approximately the point shown. Try to make these bends as equal as possible on each side. Bend, don't crease.

Flying instructions for PLANE 10 are on page 54.

Oddballs and novelties

THE DESIGN possibilities of paper airplane folding are practically endless and it is inevitable that some designs do not fit into the various categories of any book. Indeed, as time passes we begin to realize how much our idea of what an airplane should be is shaped more by tradition than by the constraints of aerodynamics, which will permit much more variety of design than we usually allow. This section is devoted to those designs that break the mold a little, and otherwise defy classification.

PLANE 11

Wind rider

THIS FLYING DISC was actually first folded by my daughter at the age of five, when she went through a paper-folding spurt of her own—alas, the malady is inherited. Although the plane looks unassuming and is not difficult to fold, it is capable of long, lofty flights, and has long been a family favorite. Of all the planes in this book, this one probably can stay in the air the longest with a single throw. On a windy day, I counted out 10 seconds of flight before the plane came to rest . . . in the top of a neighbor's tree! (Folding instructions are on pages 64–66.)

To fly Hold from below and toss forward, making short gentle throws until the plane is well-adjusted. Once adjusted, you can take the plane outdoors and make a vigorous throw directly upward—the plane will often level off high in the air for a long and slow descent. If there is a breeze, throw upward into the wind. The flight on a windy day is less predictable, but will often be spectacular.

Adjustments This plane generally needs a little elevator when folded as in Step 7. Form the elevator as described in Step 8, making short test flights until the plane has a steady, straight, almost level glide. Then you can make harder throws. If the plane tends always to dip to the same side, check the wings carefully for symmetry because a small difference in angle or in placement of folds is usually responsible. Pay careful attention to the smooth upper surface of the wings; if necessary, press out any large dimples that might have formed during the folding process. If you need to straighten out a troublesome turn, this can be done as described in the "Making it fly" subsection of the Introduction, but bend up the entire wing rather than just the back, and do so very gently, making short test flights as you go.

Folding the plane as in Fig. 7A makes a broader-winged plane with a slow, floating flight. It too can be thrown upwards outdoors, but tolerates very little wind.

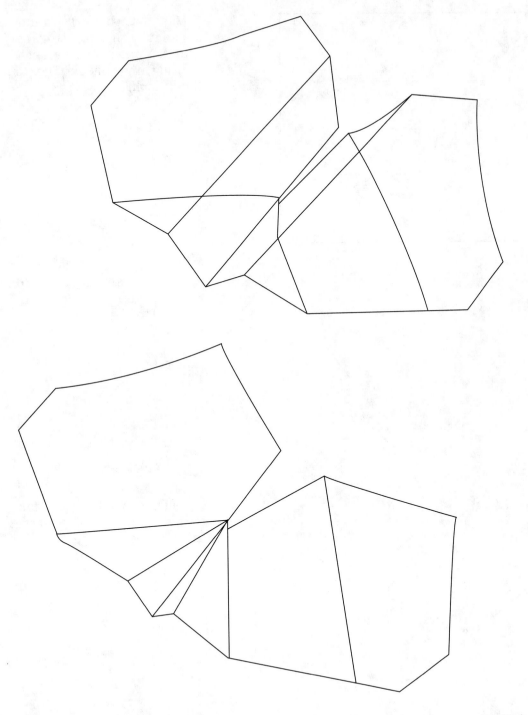

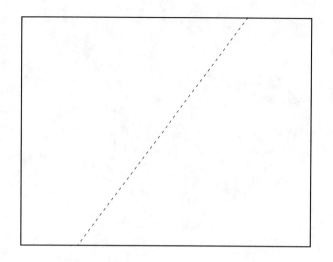

1. Make a diagonal fold as shown by carefully aligning one corner with the corner opposite, and creasing in the middle. The result should look like Fig. 2.

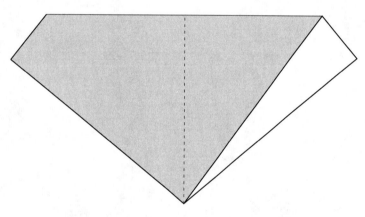

2. With the paper as shown, form a central crease by aligning the right half of the plane with the left.

Unfold.

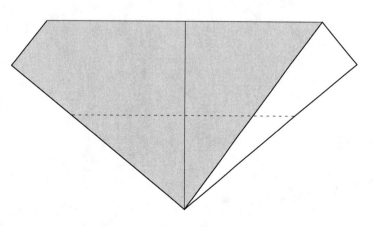

3. Fold horizontally by bringing the bottom tip up to the exact center of the top edge. Make certain the central crease is aligned, and crease very well.

4. Now fold down each wing diagonally as shown. Start your fold from the top center, aligning the top edge carefully with the central crease.

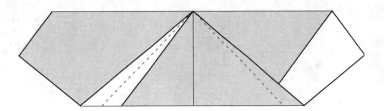

5. Shows the result of Fig. 4. Note that on the back side of the plane there is a horizontal edge about midway up the plane, marked A. Fold down the tip until it rests exactly over this point. Make certain the central crease is aligned, and crease the front edge well.

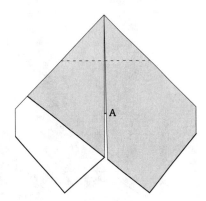

6. Now fold the plane in half along the central crease, making certain to keep the wings exactly aligned with each other.

Position the plane as shown in Fig. 7.

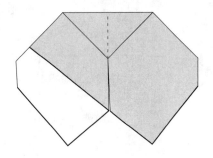

7. Fold down each wing as shown, bringing point A to point B; your fold should be just less than 1 inch from the central fold and parallel to it. (For an alternate design, fold as in Fig. 7A on page 66.)

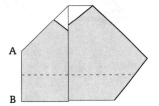

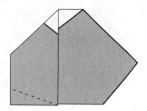

7A. Fold the wings out like this instead of Step 7 for a slow, smooth indoor flight.

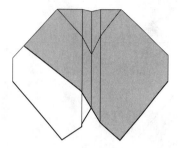

8. Shows the finished plane from above. Form elevators by gently bending up the pointed back edge of each wing.

Flying instructions for PLANE 11 are on page 62.

Bobber

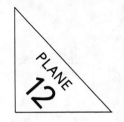
IT IS A LITTLE TRICKY TO FOLLOW the initial folding instructions on this little plane, but the design is actually quite simple. The plane is fun to fly and has a leisurely and bobbing flight motion. (Folding instructions are on pages 68–71.)

To fly

The flat heavy end of the plane is the front; the side shown in Fig. 10 is the top. Hold the plane from behind with your fingertips and push forward, or hold in your hand with the top to your palm and the front at your fingertips, and flick your hand forward to launch. Alternately, outdoors you may hold the plane from the front with your index finger in the central fold and throw vigorously upward.

Adjustment

Make certain the wings match exactly. This plane sometimes tends to fly upside down; if you find this troubling, bend the back tip of each wing upward slightly to counter this tendency. If the plane veers to one side, make corrections as directed in the "Making it fly" subsection of the Introduction, but instead of using the back edge, bend the entire wing up or down as needed.

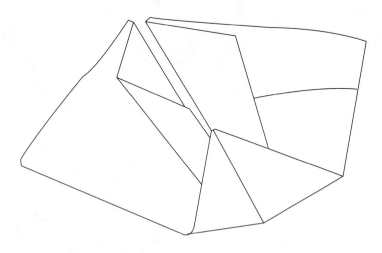

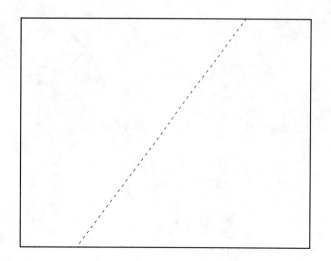

1. Make a diagonal fold as shown by aligning the right lower corner of the paper with the left upper corner. Crease well.

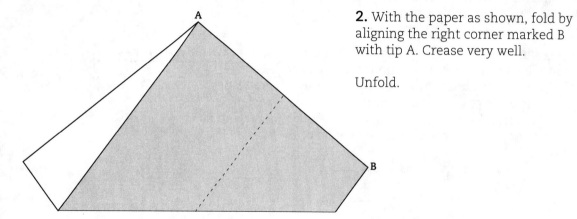

2. With the paper as shown, fold by aligning the right corner marked B with tip A. Crease very well.

Unfold.

3. Make a similar fold on the left by aligning the left corner marked C with tip A. Crease very well. (Note that both your creases should meet at the same point on the bottom edge.)

Unfold.

Unfold along the diagonal fold to open the paper entirely, folding the top half out to the right, so the paper is before you as in Fig. 4.

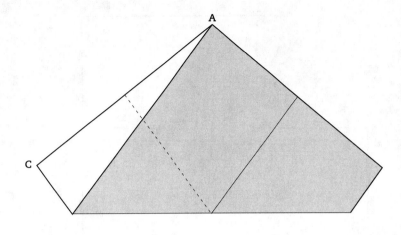

4. Fold down the left upper corner as shown, aligning the left edge with the horizontal crease. The result should look like Fig. 5.

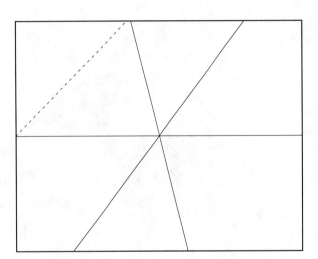

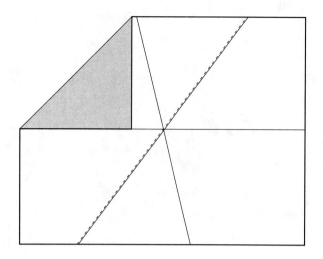

5. Now fold the right side of the paper over the diagonal crease as shown, and crease well. Position the paper as shown in Fig. 6.

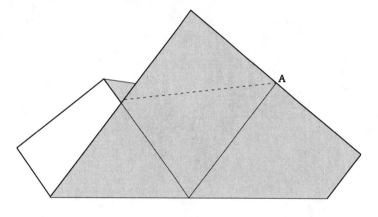

6. Fold down the corner as shown so that the upper right edge aligns against the crease ending at point A.

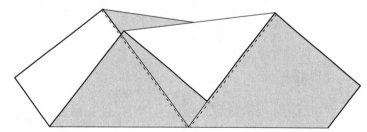

7. Now fold each side of the paper along the diagonal creases as shown. Fold up first the right side, then the left.

Rotate the paper, positioning as in Fig. 8.

8. Note that the flaps of paper you just folded are overlapping. Fold the plane carefully in half, matching the wings exactly. Crease well from nose to tail.

Unfold. The backward-pointing flaps of paper should be unfolded from each other and placed so that they look like Fig. 9.

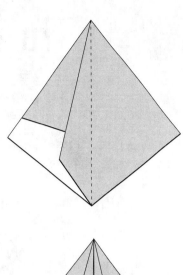

9. Note that on the back side of the paper there are crisscrossing edges of paper. Fold back the tip so it just touches the spot where these edges meet, in the exact center. Crease the resulting front edge very firmly, from the center outward.

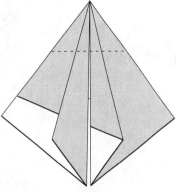

10. Shows the finished plane from above. Refold along the central crease.

Partially unfold.

Flying instructions for PLANE 12 are on page 67.

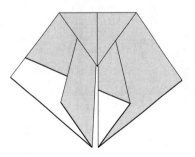

Thunderbird

THIS STRIKING DESIGN was included for its fearsome shape, which to me looks like something out of a comic book. A good indoor flier, it might even provide you with a demonstration of the phenomenon of wing flapping. (Folding instructions are on pages 73–76.)

To fly This plane can be thrown from below as were previous planes; however, it might fly more smoothly if held from behind with the index finger on top in the groove between the wings, then pushed forward and released.

Adjustments This plane might need a little elevator to fly well. Bend up the two points of the tail slightly, and try another test flight. Steering, if needed, should be accomplished by bending the backward-pointing wingtips up or down on either side as required.

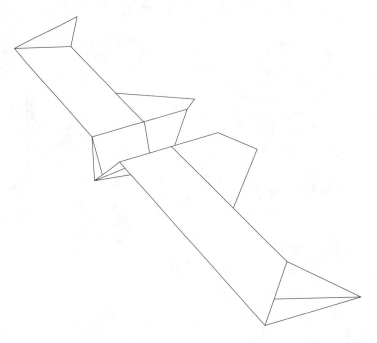

1. Make a diagonal fold by aligning one corner of the paper with the opposite corner, and creasing well.

Unfold.

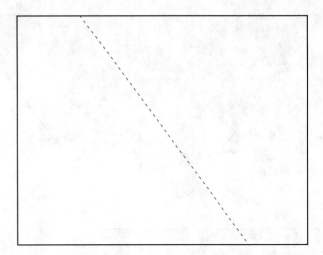

2. Now fold the paper in half diagonally by aligning the two ends of the crease you just made, labeled A and B. The fold should extend from corner to corner of the paper.

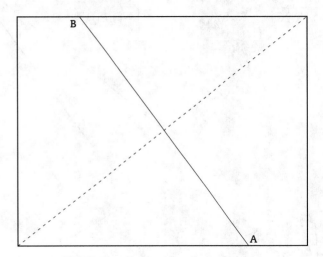

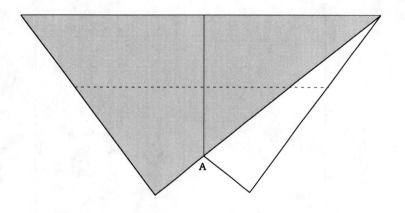

3. Placing the paper as shown, fold down the top edge so the end of the central crease just touches the point labeled A.

Unfold.

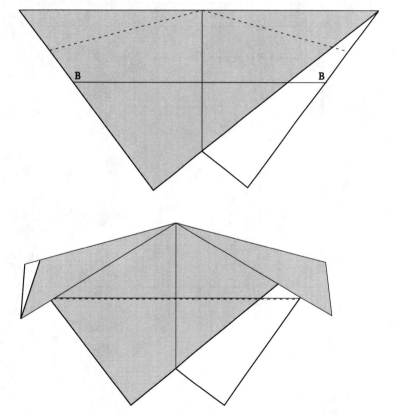

4. Make a diagonal fold on both sides of the front of the plane as follows: Secure the top end of the central crease with your finger, then bend down one wing from that point so that the front edge rests back against the end of the horizontal crease marked B. (*See* Fig. 5.) Crease well, and repeat with the other side.

5. Shows the result of the previous fold. Now fold the double-pointed bottom edge upward along the horizontal crease. The result should look like Fig. 6.

6. Now fold downward, your fold extending from corner A to corner B as shown. Make certain that the central crease is aligned, and crease well.

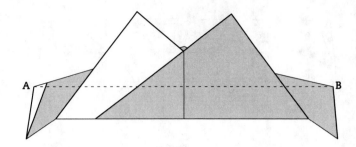

7. Now bend the tip forward so that it protrudes just beyond the front edge of the plane. Make certain that you keep the central crease aligned.

Turn the plane over.

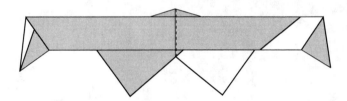

8. Shows how the plane should look from above. Fold in half along the central crease. The wings should match nearly exactly.

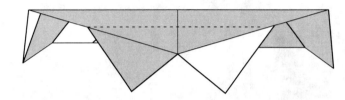

9. Fold down each wing as shown, about ¾ inch from the central fold and parallel to it.

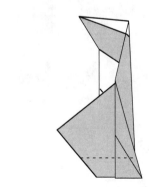

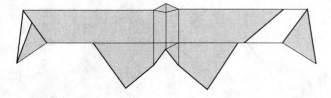

10. Shows the finished plane, from above. Carefully recrease the front and back edge of each wing.

Flying instructions for PLANE 13 are on page 72.

Oddbird

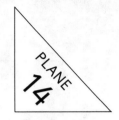

Tʜɪs ᴜɴᴜsᴜᴀʟ ᴘʟᴀɴᴇ ᴅᴇꜰɪᴇs ᴄʟᴀssɪꜰɪᴄᴀᴛɪᴏɴ. It has a simple
design and it glides nicely, though by rights it looks as though it
should not fly at all—it cannot be thrown like the usual paper
airplane. It is very easy to fold. (Folding instructions are on
pages 78–80.)

Hold the plane from behind and push forward. Alternately, you
can place the plane top down in your open palm, the front at
your fingertips, and with the hand vertical, gently flick forward
to release the plane. This is strictly an indoor model.

To fly

If the plane deviates to one side, try recreasing the forward
edge of the wings, as well as the rear edge of the wingtips.
Steering can be accomplished by bending the backward-
pointing wingtips up or down (*see* the "Making it fly" subsection
of the Introduction).

Adjustments

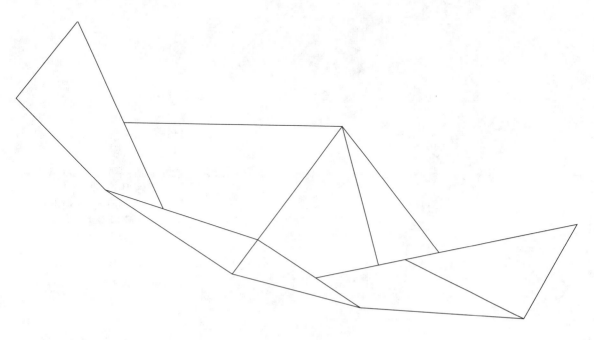

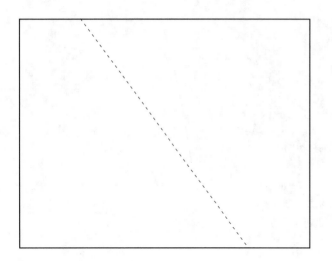

1. Make a diagonal fold by aligning the left lower corner with the right upper corner and creasing along the center.

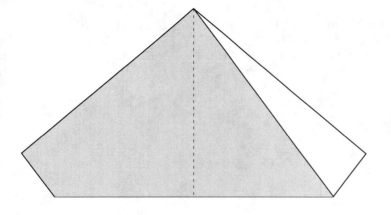

2. Placing the paper as shown, make a vertical central crease by aligning the left side of the paper exactly with the right.

Unfold.

Turn the paper over.

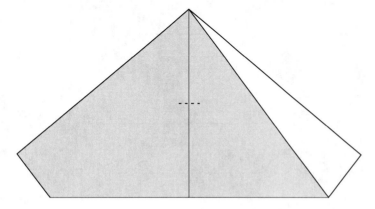

3. Mark the center of the vertical crease as shown by bringing the top corner down to the bottom edge in the exact center and making a small crease in the middle with one finger.

Unfold.

4. Fold the bottom edge up so it aligns exactly with the small crease you just formed, keeping the vertical crease exactly aligned. Crease well. Your fold should pass through the side corners, as shown; if it does not, you probably did not align the vertical crease correctly. Realign and crease again.

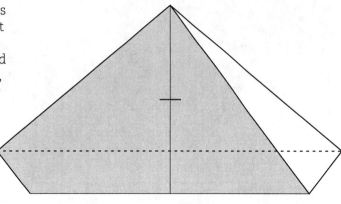

5. Shows the result of Step 4. Turn the paper over.

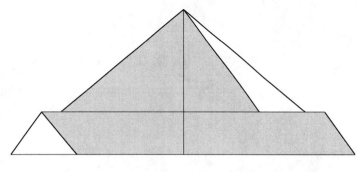

6. With the paper as shown, make a diagonal fold on both sides, extending from the exact center of the top edge to the corner shown on each side. The result should look like Fig. 7.

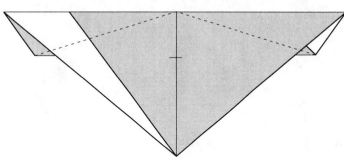

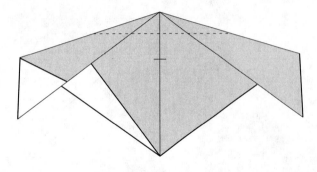

7. Find the small marking crease you made in Step 3. Fold down the tip exactly to this mark, keeping the vertical crease exactly aligned. Crease the front edge very well.

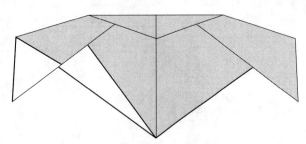

8. Shows the finished plane from above. Fold gently in half along the central crease without creasing hard, making certain that the two sides align exactly. Partially unfold.

Flying instructions for PLANE 14 are on page 77.

Another oddbird

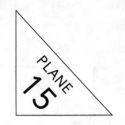

A TWIN TAIL AND A DIFFERENT LOOK distinguish this model from of PLANE 14. This plane, as the previous one, also has nothing to hold on to and so must be pushed through the air, rather than thrown. This design is especially appealing if seen from below while in flight. (Folding instructions are on pages 82–85.)

Holding from behind, push gently forward and release. This plane, like the last, will only fly satisfactorily indoors.

To fly

If you need to steer the plane, use the back sides of the wingtips rather than the tail, and follow the instructions in the "Making it fly" subsection in the Introduction.

Adjustments

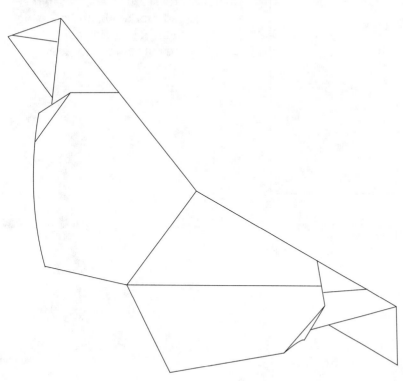

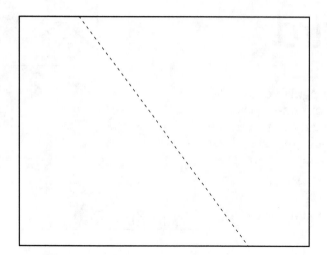

1. Make a diagonal crease as shown by aligning the left lower corner of the paper with the right upper corner.

Unfold.

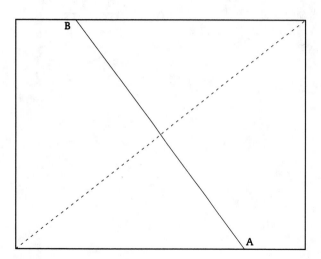

2. Make a perpendicular crease as shown by aligning one end of the diagonal crease, marked A, with the opposite end marked B, and creasing between them. This fold should extend from corner to corner.

3. With the paper as shown, fold down each corner, aligning the top edge on each side with the central crease as shown in Fig. 4.

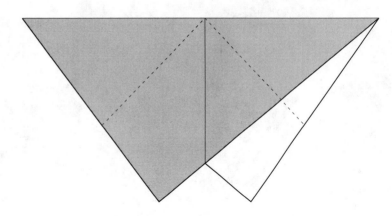

4. Note that on the backside of the paper there is an edge at the point marked A. Fold down the tip so that it rests in the exact center at this point. Crease well.

Unfold.

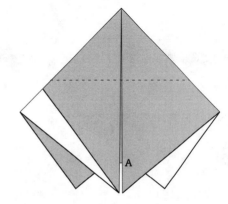

5. Now fold down the tip to rest against the horizontal crease you just made. Crease well.

Unfold.

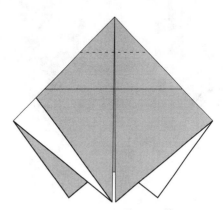

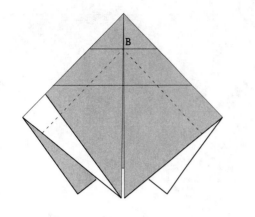

6. Fold up the wing on each side as shown. Start the fold at point B in the center, and fold on each side so that the top of the wing aligns against the horizontal crease as shown in Fig. 7.

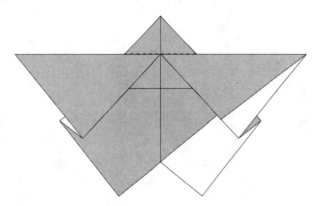

7. Now fold down the tip as shown, along the horizontal crease previously made.

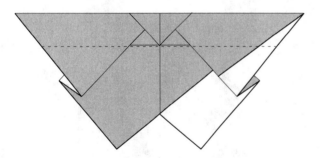

8. Fold down again along the second horizontal crease as shown, again keeping the vertical crease carefully aligned. Crease very well along the front edge.

9. Shows the result from above. Fold up along the central crease; the two sides should match exactly.

Partially unfold, so there is still a slight bend in the center.

Turn the plane over.

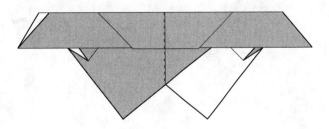

10. This shows a bottom view. Fold up the corner (shown on each side) in a line parallel with the central crease.

Flying instructions for PLANE 15 are on page 81.

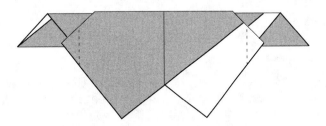

Asymmetric plane

THIS CRAFT DEFIES one of the basic principles of paper airplane design—that the left side of the plane should look like the right one and vice-versa. Like others that have gone before, it seems that it should not fly, yet it does. (Folding instructions are on pages 87–89)

To fly   Hold from behind by the diagonal back edge, push forward, and release. If your hand is large enough, an easier way is to grasp the plane by the vertical sides from below and to toss it gently forward. Use a very gentle toss and do not try to fly where there is a breeze.

Adjustments   Note that the plane consists of a base and two vertical sides. Experiment with the angle of these sides until the plane glides well. You may steer the plane by adjusting the fold in Step 7 so that the tip lies slightly above or below the top edge of the plane.

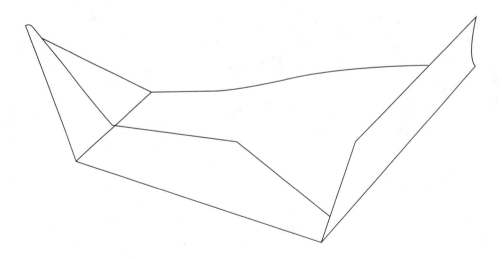

1. Make a fold from the right upper corner as shown, aligning the top edge exactly with the right vertical edge of the paper, as shown in Fig. 2. Crease very well.

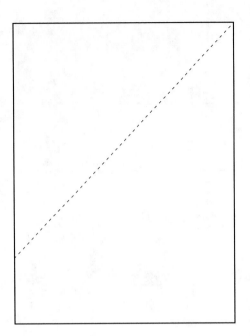

2. Fold down as shown, so that the top right corner rests against the bottom right corner as in Fig. 3. Again, crease well.

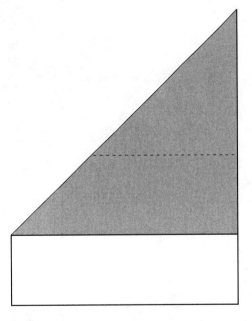

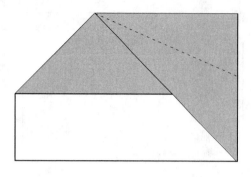

3. Make a fold extending from the top corner, aligning the top edge with the diagonal crease as shown in Fig. 4.

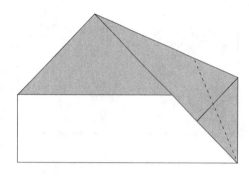

4. Now make another fold from the right bottom corner, bringing the right vertical edge over to align with the diagonal edge. The result should look like Fig. 5.

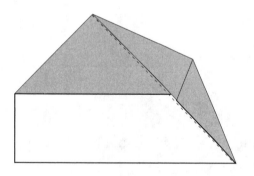

5. Now fold over along the diagonal edge as shown. Crease very well.

6. Make a fold from the left bottom corner as shown, aligning the small vertical edge with the horizontal edge. Crease well.

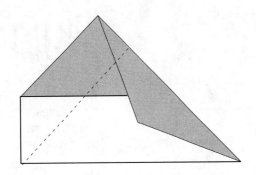

7. Place the plane as shown. With the side from Fig. 6 still folded down, fold over the right top edge so it just touches the part you folded over in Step 6. The top edge should be kept aligned.

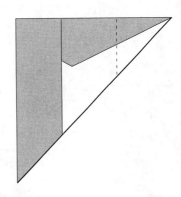

8. Shows the result. The front of the plane is to the top. Unfold partially the sides formed in Step 6 and Step 7 to complete the plane. The two sides should come up more or less square from the bottom, making the plane box-like.

Flying instructions for PLANE 16 are on page 86.

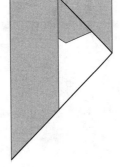

PLANE 17

Flying spectacles

Designed with double wings to look like a pair of eyeglasses, this plane is a little challenging to fold, but is reliable and eye-catching. Amazingly, it flies very well. (Folding instructions are on pages 91–99.)

To fly   With the center of the plane folded together, hold the folded part from below and toss gently forward. Once adjusted so that it flies straight, you can give a firm throw. Outdoors, try throwing as hard as you can upward, allowing the plane to glide to the ground.

Adjustments   You can steer the plane by adjusting the size of each wing opening (the glasses)—either flatten gently or widen by pressing inward gently on the wingtip. Generally, if you flatten one wing slightly and widen the other slightly, the plane will tend to go toward the widened side. If this does not produce a satisfactory flight, try recreasing the wings by flattening them and creasing the front edges and the wingtip fold, then by forming the spectacles again. Periodically, you should recrease the wingtip attachment on each side to prevent the wings from coming apart from each other.

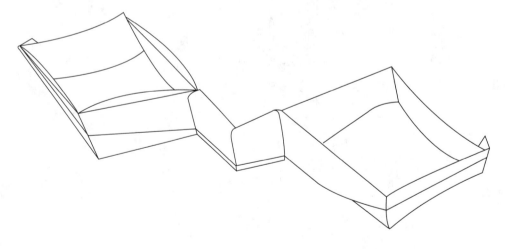

1. Make a horizontal central crease by aligning the top edge of the paper exactly with the bottom edge. Crease well.

Unfold.

Make a vertical central crease by aligning the left edge exactly with the right. Crease well.

Unfold.

Turn the paper over.

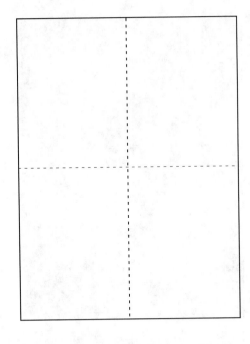

2. Now make a diagonal crease exactly through the intersection of the creases, by bringing over point A to align with the vertical crease; the result should look like Fig. 4 in reverse. Make certain that your fold goes exactly through the intersection of creases in the center, and crease well.

Unfold.

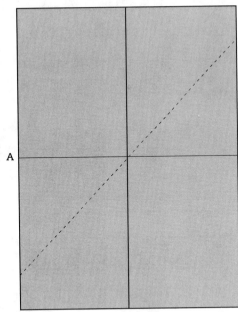

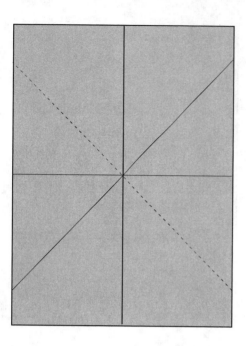

3. Now make a similar fold on the opposite side, in the same way. Crease well, but do not unfold.

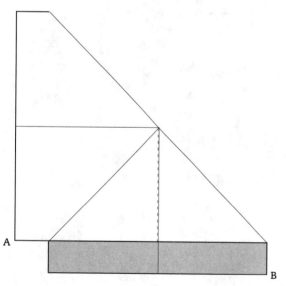

4. You will now make a complex accordion fold by bringing corner A over to rest against corner B. The rest of the paper should follow, and will bend along the vertical crease as shown. The result should look like Fig. 5; carefully line up the top and bottom layers of paper and flatten the paper well, creasing all edges.

5. Fold the top downward as shown, so that the tip just touches the bottom edge in the exact center.

Placing the folded edge over a hard surface, crease as hard as you can by running your thumbnail over the fold.

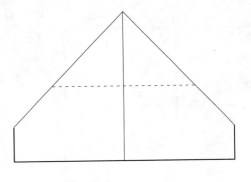

6. Fold the tip upward so that it extends about ¾ inch beyond the front edge of the plane. Make certain to keep the central crease aligned exactly.

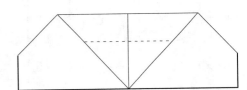

Again crease the fold you just created over a hard surface using your nail.

Now open the paper out entirely so that it is a single flat sheet, with the center bulging out toward you.

7. The paper should look like this, with lines intersecting in the center, surrounded by two boxes, one small and another large—you will use these boxes to form a telescoping fold by turning the section between them inside out. Start by creasing all around the larger box, so that it all bends in the same direction with its crease toward you.

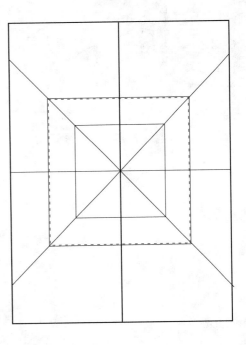

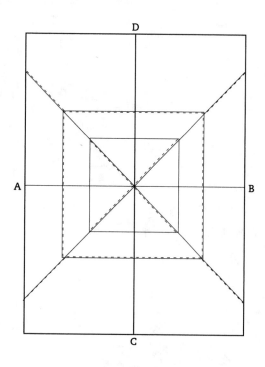

8. Now make the telescoping crease. Start by pinching each of the diagonal creases extending outward from the large square so that they bend in the same direction. The small square should bend away from you (in the opposite direction from the large square) and the center of the paper should be pointing out toward you. (In the drawing, folds that should bend toward you are indicated with a broken line.) Point A should bend toward point B in the center, and point C should bend toward point D.

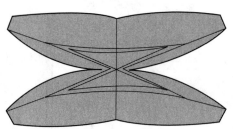

9. This drawing represents the fold in progress. Make certain that the paper folds exactly along the creases, adjusting if it tries to bend in other places. When you are certain that all the bends are along the creases, flatten the plane so that it looks like Fig. 10, and crease well. (The plane should be as shown, with a set of top wings resting directly above a set of bottom wings, and with the wings divided left from right at the bottom edge as shown in Fig. 10.)

10. Now fold the tip back along the edge as shown, creasing in front.

Fold in half along the central crease, aligning the two wings on the left exactly with the two on the right.

Unfold the central crease.

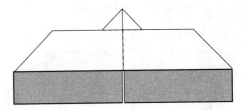

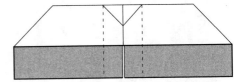

11. Fold up the topmost wing on each side from the point shown, making your fold parallel to the central crease (do this by aligning the back edge of the wing with itself on each side).

Turning the plane over, fold each of the bottom wings in the opposite direction from the top wings, along the exact same lines.

12. This is a front-view schematic of how the front and back wings should be folded away from each other. Now flatten the plane back out as it was in Fig. 11.

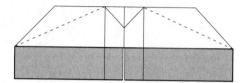

13. Fold down the front edge of each top wing as shown, making your fold from the wing fold in the center to the corner shown on the edge. Crease each side very well.

Lifting up each of the top wings one at a time, fold down the top of each of the bottom wings in exactly the same way.

Flatten the plane again with top wings resting on bottom wings.

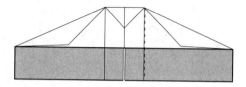

14. Fold the top right wing to the left along the wing fold.

Also fold the bottom right wing backwards and to the left, so that it rests opposite the top right wing.

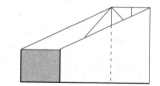

15. Fold the end of the top right wing back to the right, following the left wing fold as shown.

Match the same fold on the reverse side with the bottom right wing.

16. This is a schematic of how the right wing should be folded back, as seen edge-on.

17. This shows the same result from above. Taking hold of the tip of both right wings, pull outward to the right to straighten them.

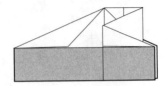

Now fold the end of the right top wing to the right bottom wing, as shown in Figs. 17A through 17E.

17A. Fold the wingtips together to the left, about ½ inch from the end and parallel to it.

Unfold.

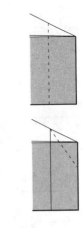

17B. Fold down the top corner of both wingtips so that they rest against the crease you just made, as in Fig. 17C.

17C. Fold up the bottom corner of the wingtips in the same way, so that they rest against the crease as in Fig. 17D.

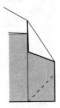

17D. Now carefully fold the remaining wingtip over and match it with the crease from Step A.

Fold again along the crease, as shown.

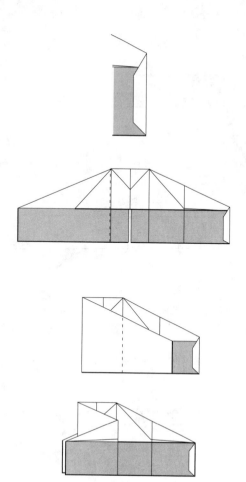

17E. The result should look like this. Crease very well.

18. Now bend the top left wing to the right along the wing fold.

Bend the bottom left wing backwards and to the right so that it lies opposite the top wing.

19. Bend both wings back to the left by following the right wing fold, as you did with the right wings in Step 15 and 16.

20. Grasp both left wingtips and pull outward to straighten both left wings.

Fold the tips of the top and bottom left wing together exactly as you did to the right wings in Steps 17A through 17E.

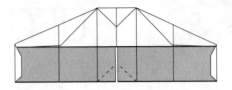

21. Shows the resulting plane from above. Fold up a tail as shown in the center on each side.

Gently fold the plane together along the central crease, forming the folded edge that you will grasp to throw the plane.

Taking one wingtip gently in each hand, press them toward each other to open up the center of each double wing, forming the spectacles.

Flying instructions for PLANE 17 are on page 90.

UFO

THIS IS A SIMPLER DESIGN from the same basic starting point. A smooth flier, it moves slowly and ponderously through the air, and reminds me of something out of Jules Verne. (Folding instructions are on pages 101–104.)

To fly Hold the plane from behind. Push gently forward and slightly downward, and release. Alternately, if you are tall or can find something stable enough to safely stand on, you may simply hold the plane over your head by the tail and let it drop straight down. It will right itself and glide to the ground.

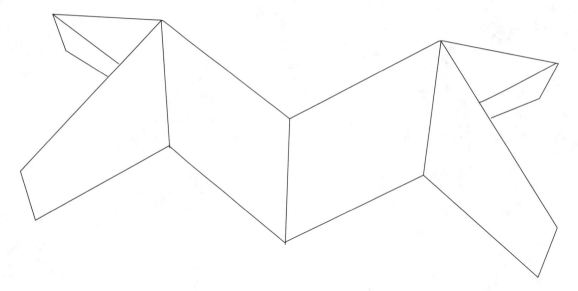

1. Make a horizontal central crease by aligning the top edge of the paper exactly with the bottom edge. Crease well.

Unfold.

Make a vertical central crease by aligning the left edge exactly with the right. Crease well.

Unfold.

Turn the paper over.

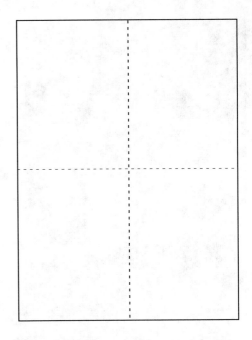

2. Now make a diagonal crease exactly through the intersection of the creases, by bringing over point A to align with the vertical crease; the result should look like Fig. 4 in reverse. Make certain your fold goes exactly through the intersection of creases in the center, and crease well.

Unfold.

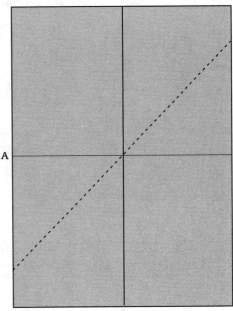

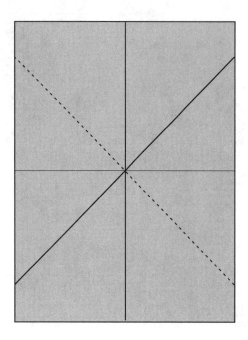

3. Now make a similar fold on the opposite side, in the same way. This is most easily done by exactly aligning one end of the diagonal fold you just made with the other end. Crease well, but do not unfold.

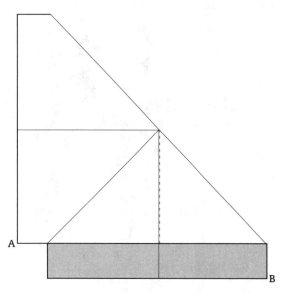

4. You will now make a complex accordion fold by bringing corner A over to rest against corner B. The rest of the paper should follow and will bend along the vertical crease as shown. The result should look like Fig. 5; carefully line up the top and bottom layers of paper, and flatten the paper well, creasing all edges.

5. Note that underneath the top layer of paper there is a horizontal edge extending from point A to point B— fold down the tip so that it just reaches this horizontal edge in the exact center, labeled X.

Unfold.

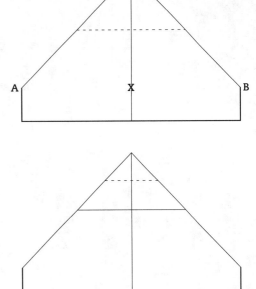

6. Now fold the tip down so that it touches the horizontal crease you just formed, in the exact center.

7. Fold down the top edge against the horizontal crease.

Then make another fold along the crease itself, as shown.

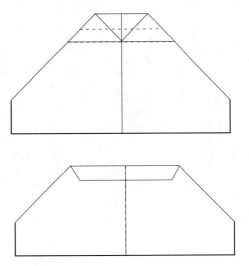

8. Shows the result of Step 7. Now fold in half along the central crease.

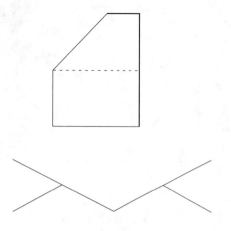

9. Note that the wings are doubled, so that there are four wings of the same shape. Bend down only the outermost wing on each side as shown, making your bend parallel to the central fold.

10. This is a representation of how the finished plane should look from the front. Recrease the front edges of the wings to flatten them.

Flying instructions for PLANE 18 are on page 100.

Space fighter #1

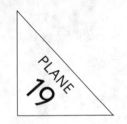
ANOTHER VARIATION on the previous two designs, this plane came to be not long after George Lucas' "Star Wars" films forever changed our idea of a good outer space thriller. Bearing a resemblance to the space ships flown by the "bad guys" of that series, it flies well and can be quite aerobatic. (Folding instructions are on pages 106–109.)

Hold from beneath and throw forward. If the plane tends to dive into the ground, try holding from behind with your index finger lying on top in the groove between the wings. Push forward briskly and release.

To fly

If the plane does not fly straight, try recreasing the front of the wings and body, and refolding the wings and wingtips, making them as equal as possible. You can also adjust the angle of the wingtips on each side to affect the line of flight.

Adjustments

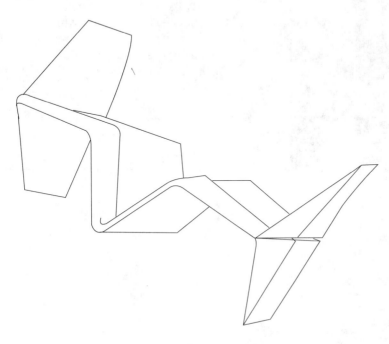

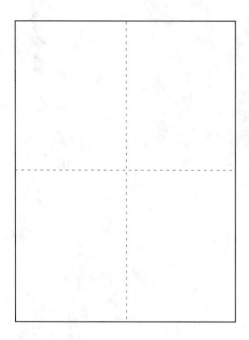

1. Make a horizontal central crease by aligning the top edge of the paper exactly with the bottom edge. Crease well.

Unfold.

Make a vertical central crease by aligning the left edge exactly with the right. Crease well.

Unfold.

Turn the paper over.

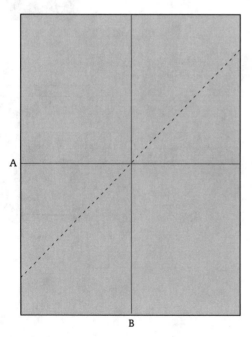

2. Now make a diagonal crease exactly through the intersection of the creases, by bringing over point A to align with the vertical crease that ends at B; the result should look like Fig. 4 in reverse. Make certain that your fold goes exactly through the intersection of creases in the center, and crease well.

Unfold.

3. Now make a similar fold on the opposite side, in the same way. This is most easily done by aligning one end of the diagonal fold you just made, exactly with the other end. Crease well, but do not unfold.

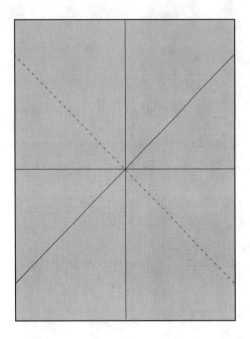

4. You will now make a complex accordion fold by bringing corner A over to rest against corner B. The rest of the paper should follow, and will bend along the vertical crease as shown. The result should look like Fig. 5; carefully line up the top and bottom layers of paper, and flatten the paper well, creasing all edges.

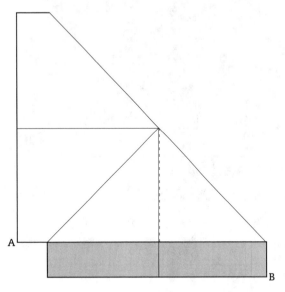

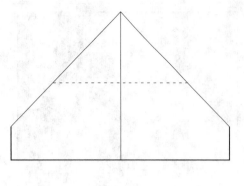

5. Fold the tip down so that it touches the bottom edge in the exact center.

Unfold.

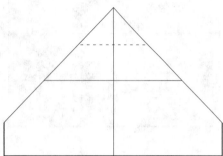

6. Now fold down the tip so that it touches the horizontal crease you just made in the exact center.

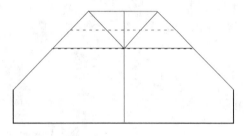

7. Fold down the top edge so that it rests against the horizontal crease.

Fold down along the horizontal crease. Crease the front edge very well.

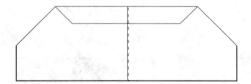

8. Shows the result of Step 7. Fold in half along the central crease.

9. Fold down the wings on each side, folding so that corner A aligns with point B on each side. Be certain to fold both wings exactly the same.

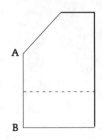

10. This is a top view. Note that each wingtip is double, with one wing lying on top of another identical one on each side. Fold up the top wing on each side as shown, and fold back the bottom wing in the opposite direction, in exactly the same spot.

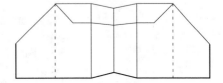

11. This is a schematic front view, showing how the finished plane should look, with the double wingtips folded upward and downward.

Flying instructions for PLANE 19 are on page 105.

Space fighter #2

ANOTHER RADICAL DEPARTURE from the usual airplane mold, this plane also looks built for forays into deep space. The folding here is quite involved, but the plane flies well, and looks out of this world. (Folding instructions are on pages 111–118.)

To fly Hold from beneath, and toss directly forward. Your toss must be very level and not hard. The plane should fly straight and smoothly. Although indoor flight is excellent, the plane will not fly outdoors.

Adjustments Make certain that the many folds are even on each side, recreasing the wings and body if need be. Steering is accomplished by adjusting the elevator on either side up or down (*see* Step 20).

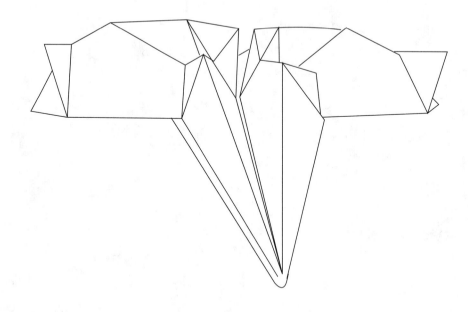

1. With the paper as shown, make a diagonal fold from the right lower corner by aligning the right edge of the paper with the bottom edge. Crease well.

Unfold.

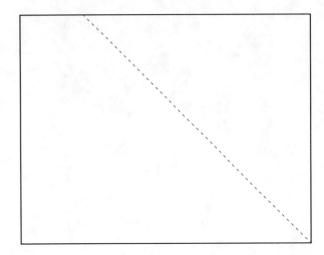

2. Make a similar fold from the left lower corner, aligning the left edge with the bottom edge. Crease well.

Unfold.

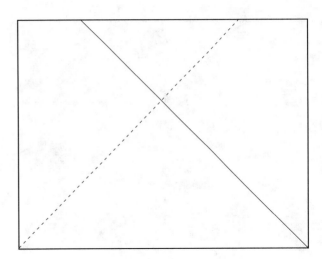

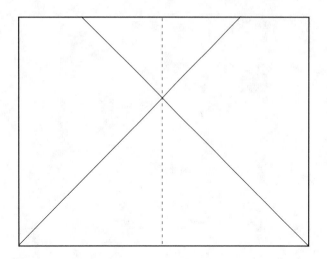

3. Now make a central crease as shown by aligning the left edge with the right.

Unfold. Note that the three creases should intersect at a single point.

Turn the paper over.

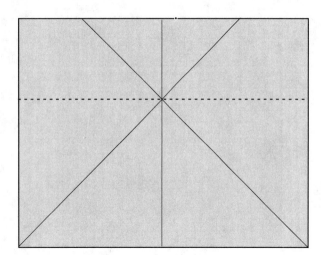

4. Make a horizontal fold as shown exactly through the intersection of the three previous creases. Be certain to align the vertical central crease exactly. Crease very well.

Unfold.

Turn the paper back over.

5. You will now make an accordion fold as follows:

~ Press down with your finger on the point where the folds cross, causing that point to bulge away from you.

~ Grasp the paper by the ends of the horizontal crease marked A and B. Bring both those ends down to point C in the middle of the bottom edge. The paper will fold naturally along the diagonal creases as shown in Fig. 5A.

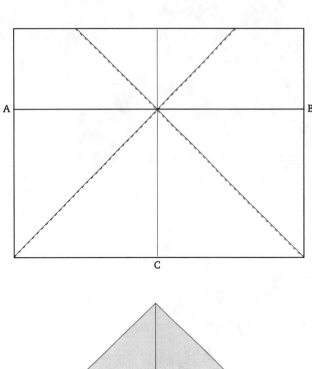

5A. Shows the fold in progress. Align the edges carefully and flatten the paper, creasing well. You should end up with a shape that looks like Fig. 6.

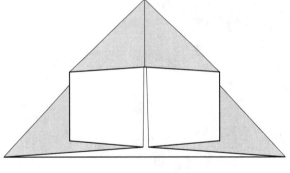

6. Note that there are two sets of wings; a small upper set overlying a larger lower set. Fold the smaller wing toward the inside on each side from the front tip as shown, aligning the diagonal edge with the central crease as in Fig. 7.

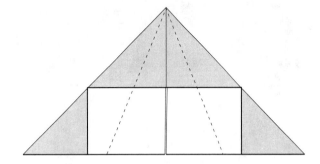

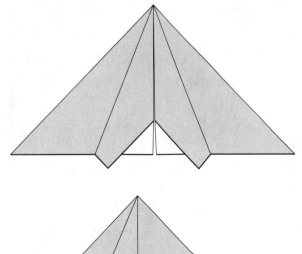

7. Shows the result of Step 6. Fold the small right wing over to the left.

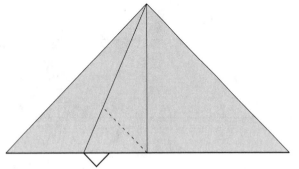

8. Now fold up the corner of the small wing on top as shown, aligning the bottom edge with the central crease as shown in Fig. 9.

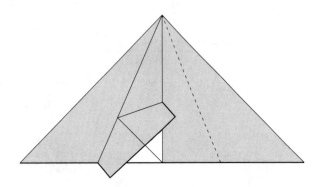

9. Fold the large right wing over, aligning the outside edge with the central crease.

10. Shows the result of Step 9. Now fold out the wingtip as shown. Your fold should extend from the point marked A to the right bottom corner.

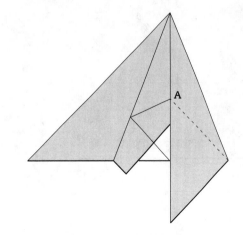

11. The result should look like this. Now fold both small wings over to the right.

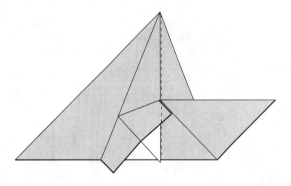

12. Again fold up the lower corner of the top small wing, aligning the bottom edge of the wing with the central crease.

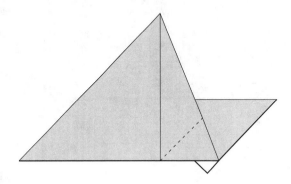

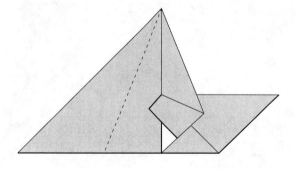

13. Now fold the left wing over, aligning it with the central crease as you did on the right wing in Step 9.

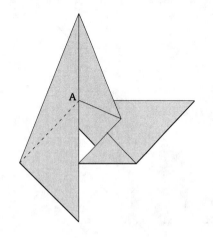

14. Fold out the tip of the left wing as shown. Again, your fold should extend from point A to the left bottom corner.

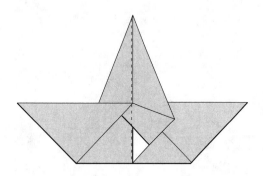

15. Shows the result of Step 14. Now fold back the left top wing.

Fold the plane in half along the central crease.

16. Fold down each wing as shown. Your fold should extend back from the tip on each side. Align the tapering front side of the plane with the fold at the bottom. Make certain both wings are exactly aligned, and crease well.

Unfold the central fold, laying the plane flat.

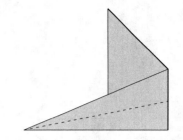

17. Fold each wingtip inward so that each tip touches point A on each side, and crease well.

Unfold.

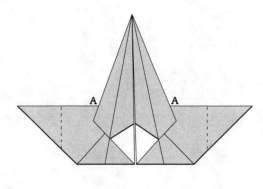

18. Note that each wingtip is formed of two layers of paper folded at the front edge. Work your finger between the two layers just behind the tip of one side, then pull the tip down between the two layers to point B. Crease on both sides; the crease will follow the line shown.

Repeat on the other wingtip. This should result in a double wingtip on each side, as seen on the front view in Fig. 21.

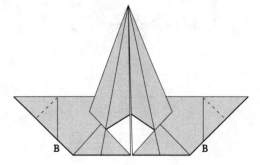

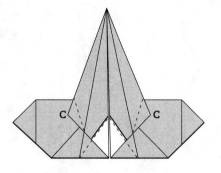

19. Fold a tail upward on each side by folding up the two corners that meet over the center bottom edge, as shown.

Also fold up point C on each side of the plane, as shown.

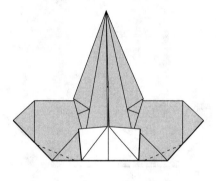

20. Shows the result of the previous folds, from above. Unfold each of them partially, so that they stick straight out from the plane.

Generally this design requires an elevator. This can be formed on each side by bending the back angle of each wing upward slightly, as shown. Bend only, do not crease.

21. This is a diagram of the plane as it should appear from the front. Adjust the folds from Steps 18 and 19 so that they are angled the same on each side.

Flying instructions for PLANE 20 are on page 110.

Things that spin

THE PREVIOUS book included a section of paper helicopters—planes with opposing blades similar to a propeller—that spin in the air as they fall. As this book is devoted to designs that are a little more out of the ordinary, we shall consider a few planes—most can hardly be termed helicopters—that do indeed spin in the air; and can be wildly entertaining.

Pinwheel

RATHER THAN having two wings, this helicopter has four, making it similar to a windmill or a child's pinwheel, which it very much resembles in flight. Folding is a bit more complex, but very worth the effort if you are up to the challenge. (Folding instructions are on pages 121–127.)

To fly Hold above your head by the point, keeping the wings spread apart from each other with your fingers. Release straight downward, and get out of the way. You can also drop the aircraft from a staircase or a ladder. Avoid breezy areas.

Adjustments Generally, if the aircraft fails to spin well or becomes unbalanced, the angle of the wings is at fault. Make certain the wingtips are pointed slightly upward, and all at approximately the same angle.

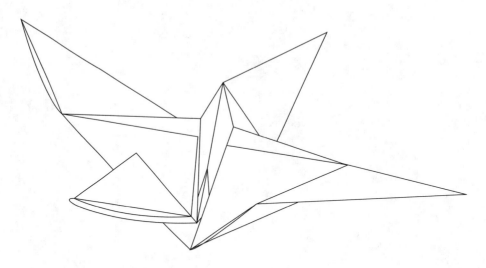

1. Make a horizontal central crease by aligning the top edge of the paper exactly with the bottom edge. Crease well.

Unfold.

Make a vertical central crease by aligning the left edge exactly with the right. Crease well.

Unfold.

Turn the paper over.

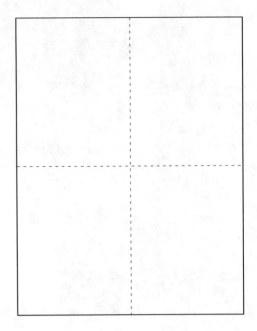

2. Now make a diagonal crease exactly through the intersection of the creases, by bringing over point A to align with the vertical crease which ends at B. Make certain your fold goes exactly through the intersection of creases in the center, and crease well.

Unfold.

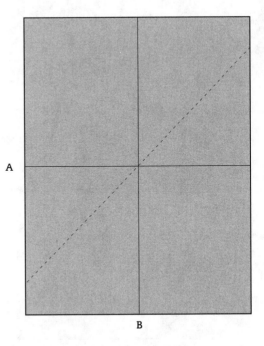

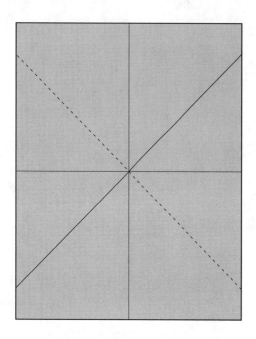

3. Make another similar crossing fold on the opposite side. Crease well.

Unfold.

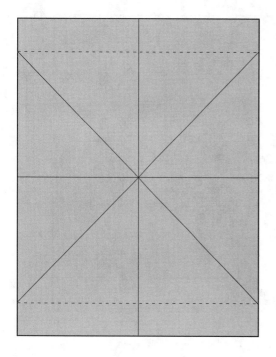

4. Now fold down the top of the paper as shown, making your fold extend from the end of one diagonal crease to the other. Make certain the central crease is exactly aligned, and crease well.

Fold up the bottom of the paper in exactly the same way. Crease well.

Recrease both diagonal folds, creasing the folded over ends with the rest of the paper.

Unfold.

5. The result should look like this. Grasp the paper at both ends of the horizontal crease labeled A and B, and bring them down to point C. The paper should naturally make an accordion fold, bringing the top corner on each side down toward the bottom corners, in the shape shown in Fig. 6.

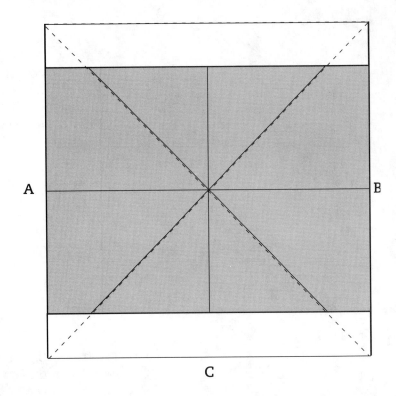

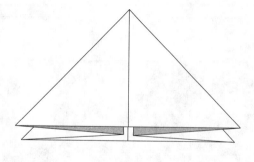

6. Shows the fold in progress. Make certain the edges are perfectly aligned, then flatten the aircraft, creasing well. The result should look like Fig. 7.

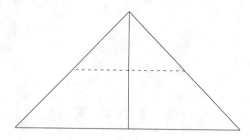

7. Fold down the tip so it touches the bottom edge of the paper in the exact center. Placing the aircraft on a smooth, flat surface, run your thumbnail firmly over the fold to crease it tightly.

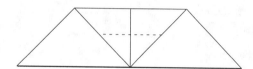

8. Fold the tip upward so it touches the top edge of the paper in the exact center. Again firm down the crease with your thumbnail.

Unfold the paper to an open square, as in Fig. 9. The center of the paper should be bulging out toward you.

9. The paper should look like this, with lines intersecting in the center, surrounded by two boxes, one small and another large—you will use these boxes to form a telescoping fold, by turning the section between them inside-out. Start by creasing all around the larger box, so that it all bends in the same direction with its crease toward you.

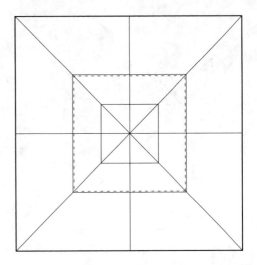

10. Now make the telescoping crease. Start by pinching each of the diagonal creases at the corners so they bend in the same direction as the large box. This bend is inverted between the two boxes, and the small box should bend away from you (in the opposite direction as the large box), while the center of the paper should point toward you. (In the drawing, folds that should bend toward you are indicated with a broken line.)

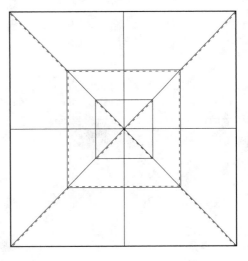

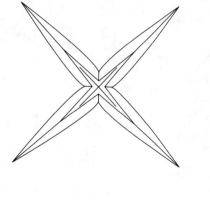

11. This is a diagram showing the fold in progress, from above. See that the center extends upward to the top edge of the paper, and align the edges carefully, creasing so that the aircraft looks like Fig. 12.

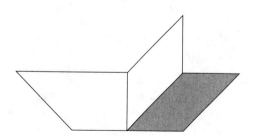

12. Place the paper as shown here. Note that you have four identical wings: two on one side and two on the other side. Fold up the topmost wing on the right, aligning the bottom edge with the vertical central crease.

13. Shows the result of Step 12. Turn the folded wing to the left, bringing the bottom left wing to the right.

Repeat Step 12 with the next wing on the right.

Continue rotating through the four wings until each has been folded in exactly the same way, always from the right. The result should look like Fig. 14.

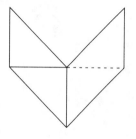

14. Now, fold down the right wing as shown, keeping your fold horizontal. Again, rotate through each of the wings, making an identical fold, always with the wing on the right. Unfold each wing partially, and open the wings out so that they are pointing in four different directions.

15. The finished aircraft should look like this from above. Be certain that the wingtips are slanted upward, so that they are well above the level of the top center of the aircraft.

Flying instructions for PLANE 25 are on page 120.

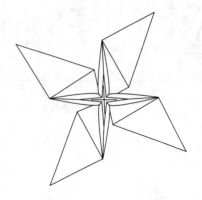

Flying saucer

Flying plastic discs have become a household item in this country, and rightly so, considering the ease with which they bring the magic of flight into any home. This design imitates the properties of the flying disc, making it a bona fide flying saucer. It might lack the range and versatility of the original, but proves that the same thing can be folded from paper. (Folding instructions are on pages 129–133.)

To fly   Hold horizontally in your hand with the folded side downward. Flick the plane with a brisk spin, just as you would a plastic disc.

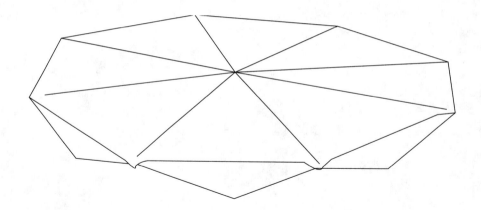

1. Make a horizontal central crease by aligning the top edge of the paper exactly with the bottom edge.

Unfold.

Make a vertical central crease by aligning the left edge exactly with the right.

Unfold.

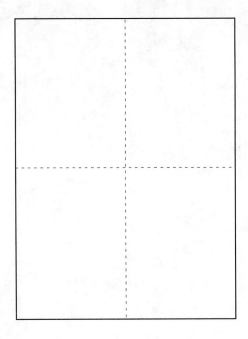

2. Now make a diagonal crease exactly through the intersection of the creases by bringing over point A to align with the vertical crease that ends at B. Make certain your fold goes exactly through the intersection of creases in the center.

Unfold.

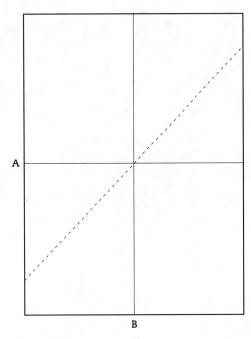

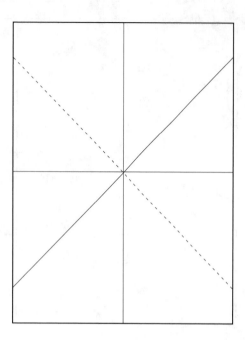

3. Make another similar crossing fold on the opposite side. This is most easily done by exactly aligning one end of the diagonal fold you just made with the opposite end.

Unfold and flatten the paper completely.

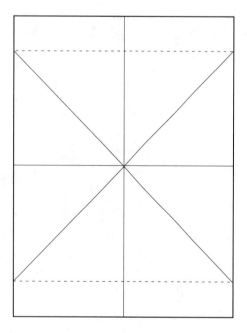

4. Form a perfect square by folding in the ends, aligning the end of your folds with the ends of the diagonal creases on each side as shown. Crease well.

5. Fold each of the four corners to the exact center and crease well.

Unfold each.

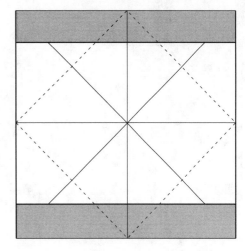

6. Fold each of the four corners so that each touches the diagonal crease from Step 4 in the exact center, as shown in Fig. 6.

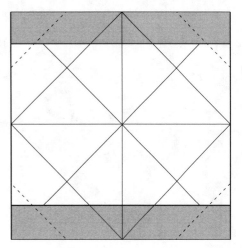

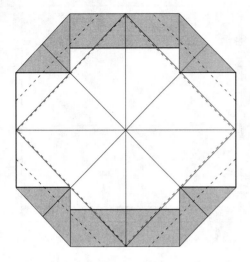

7. Fold down the edge in each of the four corners so that it lies flush with its corresponding diagonal crease.

Fold along the diagonal crease in each of the four corners, forming again a perfect square.

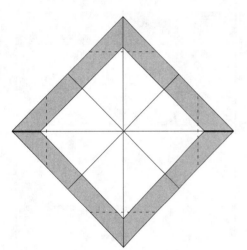

8. Fold in each corner as shown, keeping each in line with its respective crease. Crease well.

Unfold each.

9. Fold each corner down to the center of the crease just formed.

Fold each corner again along the crease. (By this time the folds will be quite bulky.) The result should look like Fig. 9. Crease each fold very well.

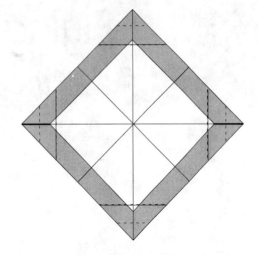

10. Note that you have formed a near-perfect octagon, with a crease extending from the center to the middle of each side edge. Bend up each corner as shown, your bends extending from crease to crease. Fold these down as tightly as you can. This is the finished saucer.

Flying instructions for PLANE 24 are on page 128.

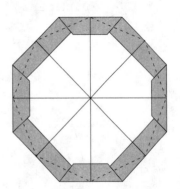

PLANE
23

Flying teacup

IT SEEMED ONLY PROPER to include a flying teacup as a sequel to the flying saucer. Thrown like a football, this little plane spins like a barrel as it scoots through the air. (Note that the design as it appears here is for a right-handed thrower; if you are left-handed, reverse the folds in Steps 4 through 9.) (Folding instructions are on pages 135-137.)

To fly   Hold in your hand with the heavy end forward and throw like a football. Alternately, you can slide some fingers into the back side of the plane, then flick the hand forward to launch the plane.

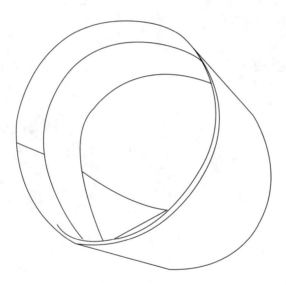

1. Fold the paper in half as shown by aligning the bottom edge over the top edge. Crease well.

Unfold.

2. Fold the bottom edge up flush with the horizontal crease. Crease well.

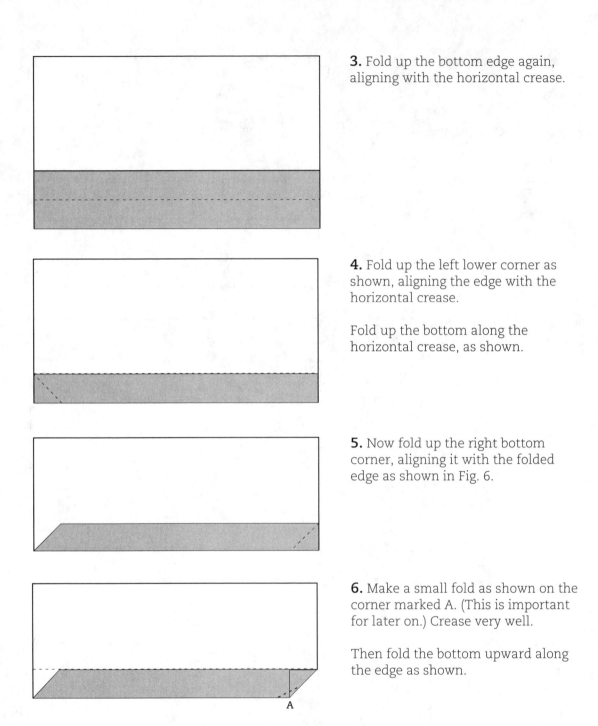

3. Fold up the bottom edge again, aligning with the horizontal crease.

4. Fold up the left lower corner as shown, aligning the edge with the horizontal crease.

Fold up the bottom along the horizontal crease, as shown.

5. Now fold up the right bottom corner, aligning it with the folded edge as shown in Fig. 6.

6. Make a small fold as shown on the corner marked A. (This is important for later on.) Crease very well.

Then fold the bottom upward along the edge as shown.

A

7. This is the result, thick in front and thin behind. Taking the thick half in your hands, run it between your fingers to make it curve upward in a circular fashion. Bend it into a cylinder.

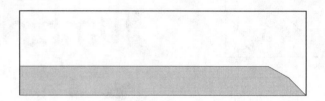

8. With the paper as shown, slide the pointed part of the front fold into the straight fold opposite, as indicated by the arrows. Press the ends gently but firmly together until they are interlocking. Then press the joint between your fingers to round it as well. (This will serve to secure the joint.)

Continue to shape the thick front end of the plane, forming it with your fingers into a circle.

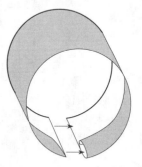

9. This is a view from behind. Fold up the loose inner corner as shown and crease gently.

Partially unfold. This small flap will cause the plane to roll.

Flying instructions for PLANE 25 are on page 134.

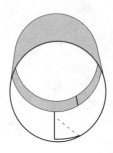

Tumbler

IF YOU HAVE EVER DROPPED a long, thin, flat object such as a sheet of balsa, you have probably noticed the tendency such objects have to tumble rapidly as they fall. This is a design that takes advantage of this tendency; rather than spinning when dropped, it tumbles rapidly edge over edge, giving the impression of the axle of a wheel. (Folding instructions are on pages 139–143.)

To fly Hold the plane in your fingertips by one edge and release, flipping the edge gently downward during the release, which initiates the tumbling motion. (Interestingly, the plane prefers to tumble in one direction, so you will find you get a better tumble launching from one side than from the other.)

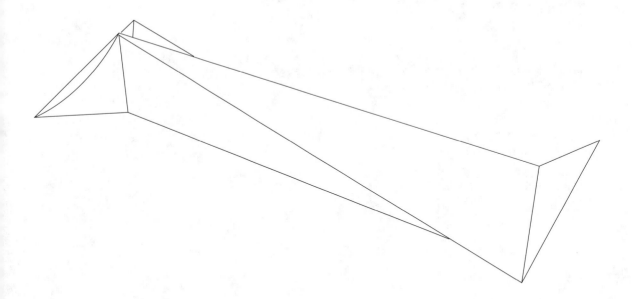

1. Start by folding from the right upper corner as shown, aligning the right edge with the top edge.

Unfold.

Turn the paper over, positioning as in Fig. 2.

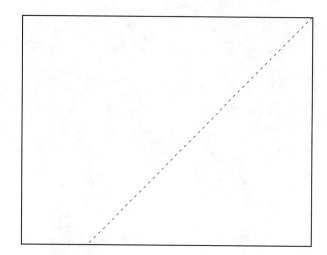

2. Now make a fold from the left upper corner, aligning the left edge with the top edge.

Unfold.

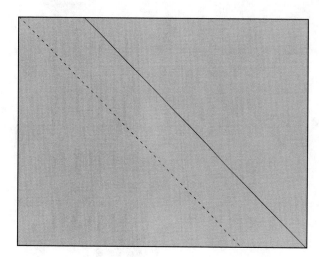

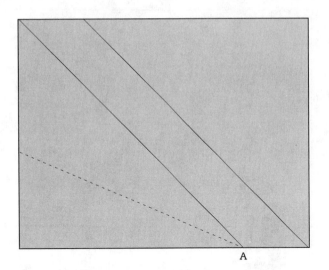

3. Make a fold starting from the point labeled A, bringing up the bottom edge to align with the diagonal crease as in Fig. 4.

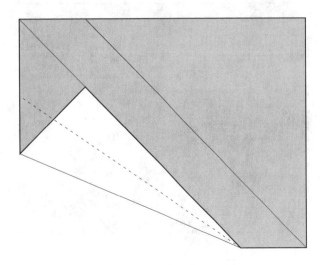

4. Fold again from the same point, again aligning with the diagonal crease.

5. Shows the result. Fold up along the diagonal crease.

Turn the paper over, and position it as in Fig. 6.

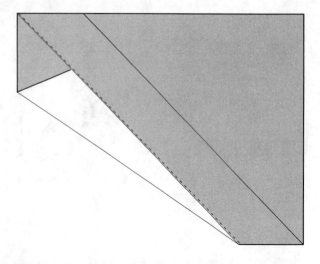

6. Starting from the point labeled B, fold up the bottom edge, aligning it against the diagonal crease.

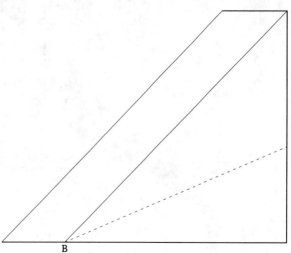

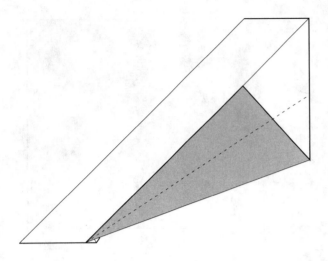

7. Make another similar fold from the same point, again aligning with the diagonal crease.

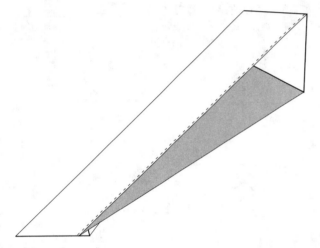

8. Fold up along the diagonal crease.

9. Fold up the left lower corner as shown, so that your fold passes through point A and the tip rests on the left diagonal edge.

Fold the upper right tip back and down in the opposite direction, so that your fold passes through point B and the tip rests behind, along the right diagonal edge.

Partially unfold both tips so that they stick directly out from the plane in opposite directions from each other. (See the drawing of the finished plane that accompanies the flying instructions.)

Flying instructions for PLANE 26 are on page 138.

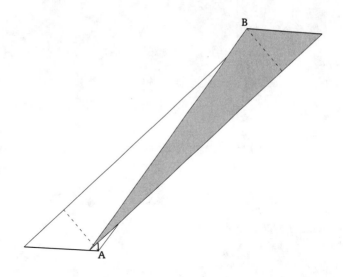